A Rainbow Book

In Praise of The Appalachian Trail Series
by Jan D. Curran

The Appalachian Trail: How To Prepare For And Hike It

"Curran's attempt at another thru-hiker 'bible' (there are several on the market) is right on the mark. If you are one of the many considering a thru-hike of the AT, a thru-read of this book is a good starting place. If you plan on tackling the AT over a number of years, or are just out for the weekend, you'll find lots of practical information, as well as good reading. Not only does this retired Army Colonel demonstrate the physical aspects of AT hiking, but he touches on the mental challenges, spiritual possibilities, and the curiosities as well.

"He has compiled the information, both positive and negative, that a hiker needs to be well prepared and ultimately successful," Isaac continues. "Browsing through this practical guide, reviewing the many aspects of hiking the AT, I was transported back many times to my own thru-hike of 1987. I certainly made my share of mistakes while hiking along the AT, and would have been better prepared with Curran in my back pocket."

— Ken Isaac, Vice President,
Tidewater Appalachian Trail Club, Norfolk, VA

The Appalachian Trail: A Journey of Discovery

". . . extremely well written . . . glowing descriptions . . . of the features and wildlife on the trail."

— NY-NJ Trail Conference

"An entertaining guide to the psychological landscape that surrounds the physical ridgetop trail."

— *Touring America*

"One of the more interesting books on the Appalachian Trail . . . If you want to experience what hiking the trail is all about, read this book!"

— *Appalachian Footnotes*
Delaware Valley Chapter
Appalachian Mountain Club

". . . this special hiking trail has again had a documented impact on an individual."

— *The MAINEtainer*
Maine Appalachian Trail Club

"This story will make the path smoother for any new hiker. The author took the time to merge with the natural world of the Trail, and there is much beauty here . . . A good book to take with you on a hike or to read at home if you haven't the time to follow the trail."

— *Keystone Newsletter*
Philadelphia Trail Club

"I would recommend this book to those who want to get a feel for long-distance hiking and insight into the Southern portion of the AT."

— *The Charles River MUD*
Boston Chapter, Appalachian Trail Club

The Appalachian Trail

HOW TO PREPARE FOR AND HIKE IT

Jan D. Curran

Rainbow Books, Inc.

Library of Congress Cataloging-in-Publication Data

Curran, Jan D., 1934-
  The Appalachian Trail : how to prepare for and hike it / Jan D.
Curran
    p.   cm.
  Includes bibliographical references and index.
  ISBN 1-56825-051-7 (hc.). -- ISBN 1-56825-050-9 (tradesoft)
  1. Hiking--Appalachian Trail--Guidebooks. 2. Appalachian
Trail--Guidebooks.   I. Title.
GV199.42.A68C878   1995
796.5'.'0974--dc20   95-34145
                                                                    CIP

The Appalachian Trail:
How To Prepare For & Hike It
by Jan D. Curran

Copyright 1995 © by Jan D. Curran

4th Printing: Updated and Revised 2002

Cover Photo: Goal of the northbound thru-hiker, Maine's famed Katahdin,
                 viewed from across Rainbow Lake (photo by the author)

ISBN: 1-56825-050-9

Published by: Rainbow Books, Inc.
                 Editorial Offices
                 P. O. Box 430
                 Highland City, FL 33846-0430
                 Email: RBIbooks@aol.com
                 Individuals' Orders: http://www.allbookstores.com
                                         phone (800) 431-1579

Manufactured in the United States of America

Dedication

To the mountain people

Other highly praised books by Jan D. Curran
in The Appalachian Trail Series

The Appalachian Trail:
A Journey of Discovery

The Appalachian Trail:
Onward to Katahdin

Contents

Foreword / 9

Chapter 1. . . . . . About the Trail / 11

Chapter 2. . . . . . History of the Appalachian Trail / 17

Chapter 3. . . . . . Before the Planning / 25

Chapter 4. . . . . . The Equipment / 35

Chapter 5 . . . . . Boots & Clothing / 39

Chapter 6 . . . . . Packs & Bedding / 47

Chapter 7 . . . . . Tents & Bivouac Sacks / 55

Chapter 8 . . . . . Other Equipment / 61

Chapter 9 . . . . . Injuries & First Aid / 69

Chapter 10. . . . . Food & Water / 81

Chapter 11. . . . . Animals on the Trail / 89

Chapter 12. . . . . Personal Safety / 105

Chapter 13. . . . . Sanitation / 111

Chapter 14. . . . . Trail Etiquette / 117

Chapter 15. . . . . On the Trail / 121

Chapter 16. . . . . Special Hikes Along the AT / 129

Appendix I. . . . . ATC Member Trail-Maintaining Clubs / 137

Appendix II. . . . Post Offices Within Six Miles of the AT / 143

Appendix III . . . Bibliography / 147

Appendix IV . . . Equipment Manufacturers / 151

Appendix V . . . . Maps of the Appalachian Trail / 161

Index / 173

About the Author / 193

Foreword

In 1991, following publication of my book, *The Appalachian Trail, A Journey of Discovery*, a chronicle of my thru-hike of the Southern Appalachians, I became aware of an intense interest in the Appalachian Trail. From all over the country, and in particular the East, people called or wrote wanting to know more about the Trail and about hiking in general.

This broad-based interest spanned generational, social and ethnic lines. Most people expressed a certain awe when talking about thru-hiking. Coupled with the awe was also a romanticism about the Trail. I sensed a longing to experience the wilderness. I'm sure a few fantasized about visiting a pristine forest and hoped thereby to experience a slice of more intense, elementary freedom. Perhaps some just wanted to taste the primeval flavor of the land discovered by our ancestors.

What impressed me most, however, was what appeared to be an almost overwhelming fatigue with urbanization. The spirit numbing commonality of urban landscape with acre after acre of strip malls, brick, cement and asphalt had clearly taken a spiritual toll.

Many looked upon the Trail as a chance for personal renewal, for the opportunity to journey to the natural world where change is the essence of reality and ultimately its beauty. Where the ability of the soul to breathe deeply is the first commandment of individual freedom and where the opportunity for solitude is its most important benefit. The emotion that sometimes accompanied the conversation surprised me.

I sensed a longing for freedom, of a desire to break out of the suffocating entanglement of restraints imposed by civilization. For a thoughtful few, there seemed to be almost a desperation to escape the banality of what passes for significance in our everyday lives.

They seemed embarked on a search for a refuge from civilization and the media that tells us all about it all the time. It was like hearing supplicants before a judge, pleading to escape an eternal punishment of daily television, trumpeting ever increasingly bizarre episodes on crime, terrorism, war and man's inhumanity to man.

The Trail offers the opportunity to test one's self in many ways. To many of the callers, I think self-challenge was a primary motivation.

Whatever the origins, the questions were characterized by an intense curiosity about the Appalachian Trail and hiking in general. At first, discussions focused on the Trail: its location, its marking, its difficulty, interesting places to hike, easy places to hike and so on. Then, the questions turned to the basic aspects of hiking. Concerns about logistics — where to get food, shelter, sleeping arrangements, where to get drinking water or how to purify it, etc. topped the list. Next came personal safety and worries about bears and snakes, and if injury should occur, how to cope.

A review of my own AT experience showed I was answering many of the same questions I had posed during preparations for my hike. Many were questions to which I had not found answers during my research. Perhaps I had not read the right books or asked the right people.

The questions impressed me with the need for an information source that addresses the concerns of beginners planning to hike the Appalachian Trail. My callers knew about the importance of proper foot wear but were unsure of what kind to buy. They believed in the necessity for first aid kits, but didn't know exactly what a kit should contain. Sometimes, callers were merely looking for reassurance or positive reinforcement of decisions they had already made, or were attempting to validate conclusions already reached. Whatever, they looked on me as a resource in trying to decide if they should hike the Trail or, if they had already decided to hike it, how they should go about it.

This book is an outgrowth of those calls. I hope it will provide some of the answers and fill some of the gaps for those who have already made the decision. For others, I hope it will provide the inspiration to make the decision. It will be a journey that, for many, will fundamentally change the perspective through which they view the world and their place in it.

About the Trail

*"Each Traveler should know what he has to see,
and what properly belongs to him, on a journey."*
Goethe

"A traveler without knowledge is a bird without wings."
Sa'Di

After a day hiking the Appalachian Trail (AT), few hikers have much interest in broadening the focus of their hike. This is understandable. Hiking in mountains is *very* demanding. By day's end, little energy, or light for that matter, remains for the ordinary hiker. Physical requirements for nourishment and rest become all consuming. All prospective thru-hikers anticipate these physical demands and go to great lengths in preparing to meet them.

What is not as well understood by the prospective thru-hiker is that the AT is not solely an arduous pathway along which one toils, oblivious to all but the terminus of choice, the distance already covered, what remains and how many pounds have been shed. The Trail also presents an exciting array of possibilities for learning about the natural world — from the geologic makeup of the earth beneath one's feet to awe inspiring vistas, fascinating wildlife, and the myriad of plants and wildflowers that brighten the pathway.

One cannot view Katahdin, for example, without experienc-
ing a sense of awe. The rolling landscape, carpeted with forests and
speckled with crystalline lakes, provides no hint of impending mag-
nificence. Then, suddenly, there it is — an imposing monolith, miles
in depth and breadth, thrusts its peaks over a mile into the sky,
dominating the earth, at least that part of the earth called northern
Maine. Why does it stand alone? How is it that for miles in all
directions no other mountains stand to challenge it?

And what of the White Mountains? And the spectacular views
across the Presidential Range from the summit of Mt. Washington,
the 6,000-foot crown of New Hampshire? Here, craggy, barren out-
crops, interlaced with alpine meadows, reach far above the treeline,
building to a succession of peaks unique among the Appalachians.
What makes them so different from their neighbors to the west, the
Green Mountains of Vermont or their neighbors to the north in
Maine?

And so it goes, the Green Mountains in Vermont, the history-
flavored Blue Ridge in Virginia, the haze-shrouded Great Smokies
boasting Clingmans Dome, the highest mountain on the AT, or the
brash, untamed Nantahalas in North Carolina. These all have dis-
tinct characteristics, as exciting or reassuring in their own way as
Katahdin or the White Mountains. Their beauty and unique qualities engender in those blessed with perspective and perception a
quest for deeper knowledge.

What produced the treeless mountain crests like Big Bald,
Round Bald, Jane Bald and others in the southern Appalachians?
Their summits, although well below treeline, contain no trees. Why?
And who was Max, the man who created the grassy massif we know
as Max Patch? Thousands of mountains, thousands of stories of
creation and change, conflict and serenity. That is the book the
Appalachians unfold before us.

What about the waters coursing through the mountain cuts,
these rivers with strange sounding names like Penobscot, Kennebec
and Androscoggin? What is known about them and the countless
others like the Connecticut, Housatonic, Hudson, Delaware,
Susquehanna, Potomac, Watauga, Nolichucky, French Broad and
Nantahala? As individual in character as their names suggest, they
reflect with exuberance or serenity the landscapes through which

they flow. What about their origins? The New River in Virginia is unique. Many geologists consider it the oldest river in North America, reaching back to the Mesozoic Period. To gaze at it and realize that its waters have flowed for 100 million years or more can be a perspective altering experience. Certainly, it provides a sobering possibility for introspection.

For those who come prepared, the real beauty of the AT transcends the purely physical appreciation of views, landscapes, rivers and mountains. This is about the beauty of another dimension. Of the opportunity to learn about one's self and one's relationship to the natural world. On the Trail, one establishes a rapport with nature from within the reality of the natural world as opposed to the one created from the abstract in a classroom or a passing automobile. The hiker has a unique opportunity to experience the perspective-altering impact inherent in the combination of solitude, time, immersion in the natural order and the beauty of the planet. It offers an incubator for reflection for those who so choose to ponder the fundamental questions of human experience. The secret is in recognizing the opportunities — and, more importantly, taking time to reflect on their significance.

To those who appreciate opportunity and immersion in natural beauty comes also the obligation to understand and appreciate its origins. Hopefully, this understanding will lead to the realization that the natural world of the AT is increasingly endangered. The population surge is producing enormous pressures for development. The result threatens to overwhelm what little remains of the once unending wilderness that stretched across the continent. Already, the pristine character of parts of the AT, located near metropolitan population centers, have become compromised, and the challenges continue to mount. Even now, in southwestern Virginia, a proposal for highway construction to support economic development threatens to change the character of the AT there. Conflicts over ski trail construction in Vermont and timber operations in Maine have recently been resolved, but others will arise.

So, with this heightened appreciation of beauty should also come recognition of the need to sustain and protect it. For that reason, if for no other, those fortunate enough to hike the AT should learn about the natural history of these mountains and be prepared not only viscerally, but also intellectually, and possibly financially, to join in the preservation effort.

Do this before the hike; once the hike begins, the physical demands are so consuming that in-depth study on the Trail is impracticable. While it can be done, the discipline required, not to mention the extra weight in books, makes it unlikely. But it should be undertaken. When one devotes six months of one's life to an adventure, it stands to reason that the preparation should also involve learning about where it will take place.

An overview of the Appalachian's geologic history can be traced back to Pre-Cambrian times — back more than a billion years. It's a story about formation of a giant land mass that encompassed the Americas, Europe and Africa, and how numerous shifts in the earth's crust broke it apart. There followed the creation of the Atlantic Ocean. During these eons, mountains rose and fell, and continents formed. Eventually from beneath the prehistoric sea, arose the landmass known today as the Appalachian Mountains. Some geologists estimate that the Appalachians were at one time higher on average than the Rocky Mountains. Over the years — because of erosion and glacier movements — the Appalachians have become smaller and continue to this day to erode.

Several excellent sources for background study are readily available. For a hiker, the place to begin any study of the AT is the book, *Underfoot: A Geologic Guide to the Appalachian Trail* by V. Collins Chew. Mr. Chew, an expert on the geology of the Appalachian Trail, is also a former member of the Appalachian Trail Conference (ATC) Board of Managers. His book, written especially for the hiker, details the Trail's geologic features. It covers geologic developments occurring over hundreds of millions, even billions of years.

Mr. Chew uses layman's terms and provides excellent charts and sketch maps to aid in comprehension. Of particular interest is the chapter, "Face of the Land." Here, Chew describes the geology of all the Trail's major terrain features. A summary chart follows containing a north to south list of its features, including a code that indicates the type and age of rock found at that point.

The Appalachians by Maurice Brooks, Houghton Mifflin Company, Boston, 1965, is also a good study. This covers some early geology pertaining to the Appalachian Mountains, but it is concerned primarily with the fauna and flora as well as specific terrain features. This is an excellent source for learning about the relationship between the geology in general and the associated plant and animal life of the Appalachians. While it covers parts of the AT, its geographic scope is broader than Mr. Chew's book.

In addition, several *Appalachian Trail Guides* discuss the natural history pertaining to their particular sections. The best section on natural history is found in *Guide to the Appalachian Trail in New Hampshire and Vermont.* It was written by Dr. John Creasy, Assistant Professor of Geology at Bates College, Roger Stern of the Appalachian Mountain Club, and Suzanne Crowley of the ATC.

Also, of great interest and very well-written is the section on "Natural and Human History" in the *Guide to the Appalachian Trail in Tennessee and North Carolina,* compiled under the field editorship of Collins Chew.

In addition to the geologic history of the Appalachians, a wealth of information has been compiled concerning the plants and animals one is likely to encounter along the Trail. Trail Guides are treasure troves in this respect. More complete, however, are the various field guides by the Audubon Society as well as The Peterson Field Guide Series. *A Field Guide to the Birds East of the Rockies* by Roger Tory Peterson, published by Houghton Mifflin, 1980, is perhaps the premier guide to birds.

The Audubon Society's *Field Guide to North American Trees, Eastern Region,* published in 1980 by Alfred A. Knopf, Inc., now in its 5th printing, is an outstanding guide to identifying and studying trees. Similarly, The Audubon Society's *Field Guide to North American Wildflowers, Eastern Region,* published in 1979, also by Alfred A. Knopf, Inc., now in its 8th printing, is an excellent source for information about wildflowers that I highly recommend.

Also of interest are the human events played out in the mountains. The Trail crosses or follows terrain features that played a major role in the chronicles of the region's human history. Trail Guides highlight some of these features and the associated human history pertaining to their sections.

I carried the Audubon Society *Field Guide to North American Wildflowers, Eastern Region.* Its color photographs aided greatly in flower identification. Although heavier than I liked, I was willing, for the sake of satisfying my curiosity, to carry the extra weight. As an aid in identifying trees, I carried a small thin, four by six inch book titled: *Master Tree Finder, A Manual for the Identification of Trees by Their Leaves*, written by May Theilgaard Watts and published by Nature Study Guild in 1963 and revised in 1985. It weighs almost nothing, and I found it covered almost every type of tree I encountered.

I did not prepare well for my hikes along the AT. I knew almost nothing about the natural history of the Trail or the flora I was to encounter. Once on the Trail, my ignorance became apparent. I have now corrected some of that deficiency, and my increased knowledge has made other visits to the Trail significantly more rewarding. It is because of this experience that I highly recommend, even for day-hikers, learning about the natural history of the Trail. This is a fascinating story, and it will make a difference in your enjoyment of the experience.

2

History of the Appalachian Trail

"History is not what you thought. It is what you can remember."
W. C. Sellar & R. J. Yeatman

Knowing the history of the AT itself can also add meaning to one's hike. This gives the Trail a personality. And it also provides the hiker with a personal perspective that produces an appreciation for those who labored and still work to keep it intact. This is the story of a vision and a struggle that continues to this day.

The AT's origin can be traced to writings in 1921 by a man named Benton MacKaye, a regional planner, forester and conservationist. MacKaye espoused a radical philosophy dealing with the industrial age, and the impact of industrialization on man and the natural world. Clearly an idealist, his work is reminiscent of Henry David Thoreau's masterpiece *Walden*. MacKaye first suggested construction of a trail through the Appalachian Mountains in an article published in the *Journal of the American Institute of Architects*. He conceived this trail as part of a social experiment to make the world more habitable. His trail would give urban workers an opportunity to rejuvenate themselves and to reorient their philosophical view of participation in the industrial age. MacKaye believed that workers should view their labor as a means in life rather than as an end in itself. And one way to achieve that change in focus was by "getting back to the land." In his article, titled, "An Appalachian Trail, A Project in Regional Planning," MacKaye envisioned his trail stretching the length of the Appalachian skyline — from the "highest peak in the north to the highest peak in the south." This trail would become a natural link between self-sustaining, separated communities developed along economic and social lines. Each community's philosophical focus would concentrate on quality of life, rather than profit, as a guide to development.

MacKaye's community network concept found little support among his contemporaries and was eventually dropped. The concept of a trail through the mountains, however, fired the imagination of many conservationists and nature supporters. The trail organizations, in particular, were quick to recognize its attractiveness for the hiking community as well as its possibilities for conserving the natural environment.

Initially, activity centered around New England's Appalachian Mountain Club, the Green Mountain Club in Vermont and the New York-New Jersey Trail Conference. These clubs focused their efforts on connecting existing trails in their states. Obviously, such an effort required centralized direction to oversee planning and operations. Consequently, on March 3, 1925, a meeting was held in Washington, DC, where the Appalachian Trail Conference (ATC) was formed to give organization to the trail effort. Major William Welch was designated as the first president.

In 1927, Myron Avery stepped into the historical picture of the ATC and the AT. Whereas MacKaye was the visionary, Avery was the organizer and the pragmatist whose genius lay in action. He became the catalyst for the volunteer effort and ultimately the driving force in making the AT a reality.

Primarily because of Avery's drive, a decade later in August 1937, after much planning and coordination, and the efforts of various hiking clubs, volunteers and government agencies in all Trail states, the Trail became a reality. Volunteers in Maine opened the last section of the Trail on the south section of Sugarloaf Mountain. The dream had become a reality!

However, the euphoria was short lived. The following year, 1938, a hurricane rolled across New England, devastating portions of the Trail. Added to that was Congress's controversial decision to build the Skyline Drive along the Blue Ridge. These two setbacks were followed by the onset of World War II. The Trail fell into obscurity. Not until 1951, another thirteen years later, would the dream again became a reality.

In 1964, recognizing the pressure from increasing development along the Trail, Senator Gaylord Nelson from Wisconsin introduced legislation in Congress to preserve and protect the Trail. While it did not pass that year, in 1968 a modified version, known as the *National Scenic Trails Act* passed and was signed into law by President Lyndon B. Johnson on October 2nd. The act's major thrust was to designate the AT as a National Scenic Trail. This afforded the Trail special protection by establishing administrative and legislative machinery to protect the land over which it was sited. The law also authorized agreements on a formal basis between the Department of Interior and non-federal groups to "operate, develop and maintain" the Trail. Subsequent developments resulted in *de facto* recognition of the ATC as an equal partner in the effort.

For those desiring a more in-depth study of its origins, *The Appalachian Trail Conference Member Handbook* published in 1988 contains an outstanding history of the AT.

Another source is *The Appalachian National Scenic Trail: A Time to Be Bold,* 1987, by Charles H. W. Foster, longtime chairman of the Appalachian National Scenic Trail Advisory Council (ANSTAC). His book covers the early years in the history of the AT. Its primary focus is on the part played by ANSTAC and the politics of major government and local players who had an impact on the Trail. It can be ordered from The Ultimate Trail Store catalogue in the *Appalachian Trailway News*, the bimonthly ATC magazine.

Incidentally, anyone serious about hiking the AT in any capacity should join the ATC. Many benefits are gained from membership, including reduced prices for *Trail Guides* and the bimonthly *Appalachian Trailway News,* among other things. However, most important, membership dollars help support various ATC efforts to protect the Trail.

The ATC national central office is located in Harpers Ferry, WV. Regional offices are located in Lyme, NH, Boiling Springs, PA, Newport, VA, and Asheville, NC. Addresses, telephone numbers and website addresses for all of the above can be found in Appendix I.

The ATC is charged to maintain constant vigilance over the Trail. Because of this, it is involved in a never-ending struggle to protect the corridor and the Trail from the relentless pressure from development. Protection of the corridor, the strip of land, ostensibly inviolate, which buffers the Trail, is of paramount importance to the integrity of the Trail system. This buffer allows the Trail to retain its pristine character. Violation of the corridor's natural environment alters the Trail forever. While the land in the future may be reclaimed, it can never be recreated.

By its own definition, the ATC is "a nonprofit educational organization representing the citizen interest in the Appalachian Trail and dedicated to the preservation, maintenance, and enjoyment of the Appalachian Trailway." Actually, it is a powerful partner in probably the finest example of effective private/government cooperation anywhere. This partnership has evolved into a tradition. On the one hand, federal and state land management agencies provide funding, policy guidance and legal protection for the Trail. On the other hand, the ATC actually administers and maintains the Trail as an official responsibility delegated from the National Park Service. The ATC is the glue binding the system together.

The ATC is composed of a Board of Managers, representing the New England, Mid-Atlantic and Southern regions, who keep a watchful eye on the entire Trail system. It coordinates the efforts of the various clubs and interfaces with government organizations at all levels.

The Trail clubs are key to the system. They are the "foot soldiers," who actually do the work on the ground. Every hiker owes an immense debt of gratitude to the individual Trail clubs. With selfless dedication, their members donate countless hours and gallons of sweat to maintaining and improving the Trail. They build shelters and bridges, hack out relocations, mark the Trail, improve water sources and keep the undergrowth at bay. Without these volunteers, there would be no Trail.

The success of the ATC and its Trail clubs is obvious. Although the Trail lies within a few hours drive of half the population of the United States, to an astonishing degree it remains unspoiled, its natural beauty preserved by the ATC and its network of 30-plus Trail clubs.

The Trail is constantly being evaluated and changed to meet new realities or take advantage of new opportunities. Basically, its design follows the crests of the various mountain ridges of the Appalachian chain. In its meandering, the AT passes through or touches parts of 14 states. They are, from north to south: Maine, New Hampshire, Vermont, Massachusetts, Connecticut, New York, New Jersey, Pennsylvania, Maryland, West Virginia, Virginia, Tennessee, North Carolina and Georgia.

The states are listed in a north to south sequence as are the Trail features. This long-standing tradition probably originated because the founders of the AT were all from New England. MacKaye was from Shirley, Massachusetts, while Avery was from Maine. Also, the north is where the Trail's first portions were opened. Whatever the origin, the AT *Comprehensive Plan* acknowledges the tradition. All the official AT guide books, as well as the *Trail Data* book follow suit. However, in recognition that most thru-hikers begin their journeys from Springer Mountain and walk north, the AT Trail guides also include a section that lists the features from south to north. This presents no particular problem to north bound hikers, once they become accustomed to reading from the rear forward in these guides.

People often refer to the northern terminus of the Trail, Katahdin, as Mt. Katahdin, because that is what it is, a massive granite mountain dominating the rolling north-central Maine forest and lake country. However, the word "Katahdin," coming from the Abenaki Indian language and literally translated, means "Greatest Mountain." Adding "mountain" to the word is redundant. For that reason, "Katahdin" is used as originally intended.

The Appalachian Trail begins in the north on Baxter Peak. This mile-high (5,267 foot) summit is the highest point on Katahdin. Heading southwest through the remote forest landscape of Maine, the Trail winds along the shores of many lakes, most with Indian names like Nesuntabunt, Nahmakanta and Pemadumcook. It crosses countless streams, among them, Katahdin, Rainbow, Pollywog and Big Wilson. It also crosses the Penobscot and Kennebec Rivers, and follows mountain ridges like Chairback, Moxie Bald, Bigelow, Crocker, Saddleback, and Baldpate.

After some 279 miles, it reaches the New Hampshire border, coming shortly to the Androscoggin River by Gorham, then heads for the White Mountains. It soon encounters the magnificent Presidential Range with Mounts Madison, Washington, Adams, Monroe, Eisenhower and others. Eventually, it works its way to Mount

Garfield and Lafayette, then dips into Franconia Notch and Kinsman Notch before climbing to Mt. Moosilauke. From there, it climbs Cube and Smarts Mountains before dropping down into Hanover, passing through Dartmouth College and crossing the Connecticut River into the Green Mountains of Vermont.

There, the Trail heads almost due west to Bunker Hill and Kent Pond. Just west of Gifford Woods State Park, it combines with Vermont's Long Trail and heads almost due south over the well-known ski areas of Killington, Peru Peak and Bromley before reaching the Massachusetts state line near North Adams, Massachusetts.

From this point the Trail proceeds through the Berkshires, Taconics, and Housatonic highlands of Massachusetts and Connecticut, drops down to its lowest point of 124 feet, crosses the Hudson River on the Bear Mountain Bridge in New York, then follows the Hudson Highlands to northern New Jersey.

At High Point, New Jersey, it climbs the Kittatinny Mountain Ridge, crosses the Delaware River at Delaware Water Gap, Pennsylvania, and begins a long journey through much of that state. After crossing the Susquehanna River, it turns southward, crosses the great Cumberland Valley and eventually reaches the Blue Ridge at South Mountain which it follows through southern Pennsylvania and Maryland, crossing the Potomac River at historic Harpers Ferry, West Virginia. The headquarters for the Appalachian Trail Conference is located at the corner of Washington and Jackson Streets in Harpers Ferry. Visit the volunteers there and prepare to have your picture taken and to write in their register.

The Trail now crosses the Shenandoah River for a 539-mile stretch through Virginia, usually following the Blue Ridge. It parallels the Skyline Drive through the Shenandoah National Park, exits the park at Rockfish Gap, then continues paralleling the Blue Ridge Parkway almost down to Roanoke. Along the way, it visits places like Salt Log Gap, Tar Jacket Ridge, Hog Camp Gap, Punchbowl Mountain, Johns Hollow and Matts Creek before crossing Interstate 81 near Cloverdale and heading west for Lost Spectacles Gap, Dragons Tooth, Sinking Creek, Dismal Branch and Lick Skillet Hollow. After swinging around Pearisburg, it heads back southeast along an extensive ridge system known as Brushy Mountain. Eventually, it reaches the Grayson Highlands, Mt. Rogers and Whitetop Mountain, before descending to Damascus, known as one of the friendliest towns on the Trail. Actually, most towns through which the Trail passes are very hiker-friendly. The Tennessee state line is some three miles southwest of Damascus, and the Trail immediately heads for the high country and Iron Mountain, the Roan Mountain Massif, Unaka Mountain and Beauty Spot. At Erwin, the Trail crosses the Nolichucky River, climbs to No Business Knob and follows Bald Mountain, Hogback Ridge, Frozen Knob and other equally colorfully named ridges. At Hot Springs, North Carolina, the Trail crosses the French Broad River before climbing Max Patch and Snow Bird Mountains.

After crossing Pigeon River, the AT enters the Great Smokies National Park and follows the Tennessee-North Carolina border for about 70 miles, much of it above 6,000 feet, before descending into North Carolina to the Little Tennessee River via Fontana Dam. It then heads for the Nantahala Mountains, Cheoah Bald and the Nantahala River at Wesser, North Carolina. After climbing Wayah Bald, Albert Mountain and Standing Indian Mountain, it crosses the border into Georgia at Bly Gap.

Visits to Powell Mountain, Kelly Knob, Tray Mountain, Neels Gap, Blood Mountain, and other knobs and peaks complete the experience, except for the last climb from picturesque Stover Creek to the summit of Springer Mountain.

The entire length of the Trail is about 2,158 miles. That figure changes from year to year, because of relocations precipitated by development or planned improvements. However, it is safe to assume that the length will remain in the 2,158 mile area, and after walking 2,158 miles, who cares if it is 2,140.5, 2,139 or 2,160 miles. The mystery and allure of the Trail lies not in its length but in the variety and the beauty of the landscape through which it passes!

3

Before the Planning

*"In preparing for battle I have always found that plans are
useless, but planning is indispensable."*
Dwight Eisenhower

Every spring, usually in March and April, a thousand or more potential thru-hikers begin a northward migration from Springer
Mountain, Georgia. Most begin with visions of mountain vistas and
burbling streams in sun-dappled forests and the dream of climbing
the awesome boulder field up Katahdin sometime in September.
High hopes!

Many do not succeed. Typically, less than 25 percent of thru-
hikers successfully complete the entire 2,140 mile journey in one
season.

The reasons for failure are numerous and varied. However,
most can ultimately be traced to one elementary factor — mental
conditioning.

Most AT literature focuses on the natural beauty, painting the
Trail with a romantic brush. This sometimes encourages the reader
to view the AT as a pathway leading from one natural splendor to
the next. In fact, the Trail does that. But sometimes there are considerable distances between those attractions. This is part of the
problem.

After a month or two, hiking can get downright boring. No matter how beautiful or inspiring the wilderness, the mind can tolerate only so many days of seeing nothing but trees, roots and rocks. But boredom is transitory and likely to be dispelled by some exceptional beauty, perhaps a deer by a stream, a stand of Gray's lilies or a hummingbird feeding on a trumpet flower.

A thru-hiker must understand that the novelty of the hike is not sustainable. There will be days, just as at home, when one lacks energy, doesn't feel very well or is depressed. The fact that the Trail is physically demanding in the extreme can add to the discomfort. At times like these, the hiker must rely on mental conditioning.

This mental part of hiking long distances provides the final measure of dedication necessary for success. In the final analysis, the will to succeed, more than any other factor, tips the balance in favor of success. And that means conditioning the mind to succeed is paramount.

It is important for the beginner to understand that hiking through the mountains for six months under all types of conditions is related to weekend camp-outs and day-hiking only in that both take place outdoors. The conditions, as well as the duration and difficulty of thru-hiking, can in no way be approximated by spending a weekend in a tent or a day's jaunt in the woods.

Weather greatly impacts the life of a thru-hiker. Parts of the Appalachians have an annual rainfall comparable to that recorded in some tropical rain forests. In fact, some have described the Appalachians as temperate rain forests. That means rain, sometimes lots of rain. And this has enormous implications for the long distance hiker.

There will be occasions, sometimes prolonged periods of time, when Trail conditions and weather are simply miserable. Make no mistake, bad weather in the mountains can become unbearable for someone psychologically unprepared. And it can be downright dangerous for those physically unprepared.

Consider walking all day alone in a downpour, then climbing into a damp sleeping bag and listening to rain pummelling the tent or shelter roof all night. Consider putting on cold, wet clothes and wet boots in rain the next morning, and slipping and sliding all day in mud and on slick rocks. Add to that blisters on heels made soft from constant immersion in water. Then, consider repeating the process for several days. It doesn't take long under such conditions before most hikers begin to question why they are subjecting themselves to such misery.

Almost everyone in reasonably good health, who contemplates thru-hiking the Trail, can handle it physically. Yes, time is required to become conditioned to the actual physical demands, but that process, depending on level of fitness at the start, will not last more than a couple of weeks or a month at the most. After getting fit, the hiker has only to be prudent about the physical demands placed on the body, and the rest will take care of itself. With mental conditioning, the process is different. This is a continuing process, and the hiker should recognize the difference and be prepared for the effort involved.

Mental conditioning will be affected by the decision whether to hike solo or with a partner or partners. While there are advantages and disadvantages in both, most knowledgeable Trail people recommend, for security purposes, hiking with a partner. However, this is not the right decision for everyone.

Some thru-hike alone for a sense of independence. Others want to challenge themselves, to test their mettle to hike long distances in the wilderness alone. They want to know if they have the fortitude to handle it. Hiking alone, naturally, is most mentally demanding. Hiking for days by one's self can be very lonely.

Most hikers enjoy the comradeship and satisfaction of sharing their experience with another. Some simply feel uncomfortable when alone for long periods. They need human companionship. This depends entirely on the personality of the individual thru-hiker and his or her goals.

I have hiked both ways. My first summer, I found that the solitude of solo hiking allowed complete concentration on some important facets of my life. This led to changes in my life's most fundamental priorities. I also found that often, although I was hiking solo, I wasn't alone. I encountered many other hikers.

Many solo thru-hikers eventually form informal partnership arrangements with other solo thru-hikers. This is particularly true if the hiker begins in early spring with the great wave of northbound hikers. One just naturally falls in with hikers of similar pace.

During my second summer on the Trail, I hiked with a partner. This impacted on my ability to meditate. But I learned that
companionship had become more important than meditation. When
my partner left to return to work, I became lonely, and it was more
difficult to maintain my enthusiasm for the hike.

A realistic self-appraisal is necessary to decide whether or not
to thru-hike alone. The most important questions to ask are:

Am I comfortable being by myself for six months under trying physical conditions with little human contact?

Are my temperament and personality such that I can withstand the mental stress of being alone for an extended period?

Do I really like myself?

These may seem like elementary questions; however, if one
requires extensive external psychological support during difficult
periods in life, one will have difficulty hiking alone for prolonged
periods. If such is the case, seeking the company of a partner may
be the answer.

Those I know who have thru-hiked alone appeared to have
four things in common. First, all were uncommonly independent.
Second, bad weather or poor trail conditions had little effect on
them. Third, all were totally committed to their hike. Finally, most
were somewhat introverted.

Conversely, those not finishing their hikes, with few exceptions, had unrealistic expectations. They were unable to adapt to
changing conditions, to accept, that upon entering nature's domain,
it was they who had to adjust. Also, many had negative mindsets
and complained frequently.

The point is, the solo thru-hiker must condition the mind. One
must recognize that there will be occasions, sometimes prolonged
periods, when one's commitment will be severely tested. Though
difficult, the thru-hiker must be prepared to work at maintaining a
positive mental attitude.

One must commit to a thru-hike goal — to continue no matter what. And if the situation becomes so bleak one is tempted to
give it up, one should come off the Trail for a day. Check into a
motel. Indulge in a hot shower, a good dinner, a soft bed with real
sheets and pillows. Then, head back to the Trail. A technique I
found useful in maintaining a positive outlook during periods when

the weather and injuries began sapping enthusiasm was to shift my focus to the environment. Remain focused on the positive aspects of the hike, even if you have to manufacture them at the time.

The simple act of putting a pack on your back and heading into the woods, transports you to another world. You have now entered nature's domain. This is significant; you have surrendered external control of events to nature. *You* must adapt to the situations created by weather and terrain. The elements are neutral. They come and go, according to rules that you are powerless to influence.

But this does not mean you have no influence. You have the power to influence yourself. You have the natural human ability to adapt. You can, if you choose, delay the hike for the day and wait until the situation improves, or you can recognize that conditions are temporary and shift your focus to some positive aspect of your hike. You can simply will yourself to ignore the physical discomfort and concentrate instead on your inner strength.

The mountains, even in miserable weather, have a special beauty. In finding that beauty, you will be infinitely richer for the experience. Anyone can complain, but it takes the special person to step back and look at the situation from a different perspective or in a different light. In the final analysis, you are responsible for your reactions. If you acknowledge this, all else becomes easier. Assume responsibility, and you will be halfway up Katahdin.

Conversely, for many, thru-hiking with a partner has decided advantages over hiking solo. First, there is psychological reassurance in knowing you are not alone, that someone is there in an emergency. Second, companionship can be invaluable in facing challenges. And having someone with whom to share the experience can make the adventure more enjoyable. Many thru-hiker partnerships evolve into lifelong friendships.

Finding a partner for a thru-hike is not easy. Where does one find someone who can drop a career and wander in the woods for six months? Rarely can one find a partner from within their circle of friends and acquaintances.

While advertising in the local newspaper is a possibility, a better place to look would be with the various Trail-maintaining organizations belonging to the Appalachian Trail Conference. These all have bulletin boards and most publish newsletters. A list of clubs with telephone numbers and addresses can be found in Appendix I at the back of this book. Another source might be your local hiking club.

Still another place is the "Public Notices" of the *Appalachian Trailway News* which contains a section called, appropriately enough, "Hiking Partners." You can either advertise yourself or respond to advertisements. These usually list age, capabilities, gender, anticipated hiking speed and distance to be covered.

The thru-hiker should be aware that hiking with a partner is no guarantee of trouble free hiking or of success. The reality is that the partners will continue in close personal contact long after the novelty of the wilderness fades. Be aware, frictions develop easily during times of discomfort and fatigue. Sometimes difficulties overwhelm the partnership. I have seen several partnerships degenerate into such unbearable situations that both partners left the Trail.

Choose your partner carefully. Each must understand exactly the other's expectations. Make sure your physical abilities are roughly comparable; or plan to cooperate and compromise to reduce the differences. If your paces are different, plan to hike separately. Meet at predetermined points for breaks or lunch. Or allow the faster partner to carry more weight. Like handicapping a race horse, this tends to equalize the outcome, and if the faster person doesn't object, it'll work. I prefer to slow down, if the pace is not too slow, or to meet at a prearranged location.

If you do decide to hike with a partner, initially each should be independently equipped in case the partnership unravels. Once the partnership is firmly established, you can negotiate share-carrying of common items: tent, stove, cook kit, fuel, water bag, etc. That can significantly reduce the weight carried by each.

Some people have habits or idiosyncrasies (like loud snoring) that others find irritating, if not offensive. If your partner's habits offend you or vice versa, this can soon become a major issue.

It is imperative that partners recognize that each is entitled to hike "their own hike." They must be considerate of the other's "space" and privacy. Silent time for private thoughts can be very important. With so much togetherness, partners need to be sensitive to behavior signalling resentment or irritation.

When these arise, immediately discuss the issue. In most cases, that will be enough to resolve it. Finally, be tolerant. Both partners are human and will certainly do or say things that irritate. *The secret is to recognize the other's humanity.*

Physical and mental conditioning are interdependent. One who is not mentally fit will not complete their hike, and one who is not physically fit will adversely affect his psychological approach to the hike. *Physical conditioning is crucial.*

How can you prepare physically to hike the notoriously demanding Appalachian Trail? My usual laughing response is to say, "Nothing prepares one to hike long distances in the mountains, other than hiking long distances in the mountains." While that comment contains more than a grain of truth, it does not tell the whole story.

A survey of AT thru-hikers by Roland Muesser in 1989 found that a hiker's physical condition affected the first 30 days of the hike. After that, everyone was equally conditioned — a significant statistic. These first 30 days represent 18 percent of the entire hike, so make it as pleasant as possible. Conditioning is important!

Therefore, every thru-hiker, or any hiker for that matter, should become as physically fit as possible prior to beginning the hike. Dunham Gooding, a president of the American Alpine Institute, said it succinctly: "The more fit you are, the more fun you have. You want to be focused on the things you're out there to see, not just the sufferings of your body." Good advice!

Develop a conditioning plan. Start your program early. Set your start date and begin to train at least a couple of months before. Start slowly and work gradually toward your intended level of fitness. Too much, too fast is a recipe for injury. Allow your body time to adjust to the new demands you place on it. Your goal should be to exercise continuously for a couple of hours without undue fatigue.

Use exercises that contribute specifically to hiking. If you live in an area with hills, add climbing them to your exercise plan. However, if you live in a flat area like Florida, climb stairs in a tall building. Clearly, stair climbing is less than exciting and people will look at you oddly. But, remember, building muscles counts, not someone else's thoughts. If you have access to a stair-stepping machine, use it if you can't train outdoors.

Again with stairs or a stair-stepping machine, the watchword is start slowly. Work out for four to six weeks initially to get fit. About two or three weeks prior to beginning your hike, add hiking boots and the pack to achieve your desired level of fitness. Load the backpack with at least the weight (50 pounds is a good figure) you plan to carry on the hike, go into the woods and walk around for several hours. While you're there, look at wildflowers, notice the birds and animals. Continue this on a regular, programmed basis.

Also, consider doing wind-sprints and jogging to help in cardiovascular conditioning. A few trips to a weight room are good for developing the upper body strength needed to manhandle your pack.

If possible, spend some time walking barefoot to toughen the soles of your feet. I walked the beach in bare feet for an hour each day for three weeks. I experienced no problems with blisters, at least on the soles of my feet. I did have a problem with blisters caused by boots rubbing against my heels. But that was an equipment problem, not one of conditioning.

With proper training, the time required to become fully conditioned to the rigors of the Trail can be significantly reduced. But rarely will a hiker be fully conditioned when initially stepping onto the Trail.

A major problem is that many beginners fail to understand this. They often try to do too much the first day. The result is damaged or weakened muscles and ligaments, and sometimes major injury. Then, of course, the hiker has to abort the hike.

On the Trail, as in training, one should follow the rule of "gradualism." Start slowly — that means walk slowly. For the first day, stop early — after only a few miles, perhaps less than six or seven, or even fewer, depending on the demands of the terrain. Increase the distance the next day, still taking it easy. Seven or eight miles are sufficient. On the third day, increase the distance to whatever feels comfortable but certainly not more than ten miles. After that, you are your own best guide. Remember, resist the tendency to push your limits.

Remember, also, that age is a factor. The older the hiker, the more care needs to be taken in conditioning. Recovery times become increasing longer as one ages. It is even more important for older people to observe the "gradualism" rule.

I have met several hikers, young and old, returning to the Trail after recovering from injuries suffered the previous year. Almost all recounted that they had overdone it the first day, injured a knee or an ankle, and had to abort their hike. And to make matters worse, they continued to be affected, even a year later, by the injury. Remember, your goal is to enjoy an adventure, not take a trip on a stretcher.

4

The Equipment

"He who would travel happily must travel light."
Saint Exupery

Everyone has camping equipment stashed in the basement, attic or garage. The natural inclination for anyone planning a hike is to haul it out and clean it up. First come the old lug-sole wafflestompers, then the Army surplus knapsack. Throw a blanket or two in it and hang a Daniel Boone bear skinnin' knife from your belt, and you're ready to head out. Wrong!

Hiking long distances in the mountains is unrelated to Army style bivouacs. Hikers need backpacking equipment: functional, rugged, lightweight equipment. The key words are functional, rugged and lightweight. Remember, a thru-hiker's equipment will be subjected to prolonged use and abuse in all types of weather and temperatures, under conditions that one can scarcely imagine. It still must function during the climb of that last mountain. And the hiker must be able to get it to that last climb. That is the function of lightweight, light enough to carry and still allow one the energy to walk and climb mountains for ten hours or more a day over a period of months.

Seldom will the prospective thru-hiker have all the necessary equipment sitting around the house. Obviously, that means equipment purchases. Many hikers carry hundreds, some thousands, of dollars in equipment. With such large amounts of money at stake, it is important to approach equipment purchases with great care. Invest as much time in the study and evaluation of hiking equipment as in making any large purchase.

Much of the equipment a hiker chooses to carry is a matter of personal preference. I have met thru-hikers who carried no stoves. For suppers, they rehydrated freeze-dried food by adding water to the food pouch in the morning, carried it throughout the day and hoped it would be edible at supper. In the evening, the process was repeated for breakfasts. Some thru-hikers carried no tent, only a plastic sheet or a tarp for makeshift shelter in emergency situations.

One man had a full two-gallon can of Coleman fuel dangling from his pack. Another hiker had a fishing rod, poking through the top of his pack. Still another strapped a multicolored, golfing umbrella to his pack frame. Others carried radios and even TV cameras. Several carried miniature cassette recorders to record the highlights of their adventure. Most carried trail journals for that purpose too.

The point is: You can carry whatever you wish, so long as you can bear the weight. There are no rules about what you carry. But, your equipment must meet certain requirements. It must provide you with sufficient nourishment and fluids, allow you to sleep properly and maintain your body in a healthy condition. How you do that and what extras you carry, are strictly personal preferences.

However, almost every hiker satisfies these requirements by purchasing standard camping items, starting with clothing and boots. Packs and sleeping gear are close behind. Next are tents and cook stoves. After these basics are items like toiletries, first aid equipment, flashlights and knives.

Prospective thru-hikers should prepare a list of equipment and food they plan to carry. My first list contained: clothes, boots, a pack, a tent, a sleeping bag, a sleeping pad, a stove with fuel, cookpots, dishes, a cup, silverware, a water canteen, a first aid kit, toilet articles, a flashlight, insect repellant, maps and guidebooks, a pocket knife, Bic lighters for fire starters, matches, and food. A classification of twenty-one items in all.

After making your list, discuss it with other hikers, preferably thru-hikers. Then, test it. Take it out on a trial hike. Work out kinks or glitches. Do this well in advance to allow for the time and flexibility to modify your list and upgrade or replace items before starting your hike. If you find, as I did, that certain items do not meet your performance expectations, replace them. In my case, a stove and a flashlight were problems, and they shortly became history. On the advice of another thru-hiker, I added a water bag, a pack cover, a water filter and sandals for wear around camp.

I quickly learned that plastic garbage bags and Ziploc plastic bags were very useful; I always carried several extras. Ziploc bags stored items like toilet paper and kept matches dry. Garbage bags can be used as temporary pack covers in a heavy rain or as waterproof containers for sleeping bags. I added a plastic scrubber for cleaning cooking and eating utensils, and a dishcloth, both of which I also carried in Ziploc bags. You will discover other uses for plastic bags.

If you decide to use items rescued from the attic or garage, check them out well in advance. Many times these items need repair or cleaning. Follow manufacturers directions, since some items require special treatment.

For example, don't dry clean articles made of Gore-Tex. Dry cleaning fluids damage the material's water-repellant properties and cause leaks. Instead, use cold water and a powdered detergent. Don't use bleach. Wash by hand or on the gentle cycle in the machine. For closed-cell foam or open-cell foam rubber pads, wash with a mild soap and lay flat to dry. For air mattresses, inflate and check for leaks. In older mattresses, leaks may develop around the valves. Holes in fabric or rubber may be repaired using a patch kit.

Stoves require particular attention. Carefully remove carbon buildup. Inspect gaskets and O-rings, and replace if they show any signs of dryness or cracking. Follow manufacturers' instructions. Lightly oil any moveable metal parts. If, after all your efforts, the stove does not function 100 percent, replace it.

Wash all clothing. Hand wash woolen garments with liquid soap in cold water and lay out on towels to dry as you would sweaters. Cotton and mixed cotton/synthetic material can be washed on the normal cycle. Fleece and pile items should be washed on the machine's gentle cycle. Brush these items as they dry to reduce pilling. Tumble drying on low heat is also effective to reduce pilling.

Special care should be exercised when washing polypropylene (polypro) garments or equipment. The low melting point of polypro makes it especially vulnerable to damage from high heat settings. Also, polypro has a reputation for retaining body odor, so it may require more than one washing in lukewarm or cold water to remove body odors from the fabric.

Many bargain hunters try to reduce costs by purchasing used equipment. That is generally not a good idea when outfitting for a thru-hike. However, if you insist, question the owner closely. Determine why he is selling. But most importantly, test the equipment before making payment.

I recommend that those outfitting for a six-month thru-hike buy new, quality, brand-name gear from a reputable dealer. If it is defective in any way, or it breaks down, the item will be easier to replace or get repaired. Also, it will probably cost less in the long run. Meanwhile, there will be less chance of breakdown on the Trail where replacement or repair is most difficult.

Succeeding chapters cover the basic categories of hiking equipment. Included is a discussion of the major considerations a buyer should review in making a selection. Remember, price should not always be the deciding factor in equipment selection. However, you usually get what you pay for. Equipment bought at cut-rate prices in discount houses will rarely stand up to the punishment of a thru-hike.

Recreational equipment companies are constantly improving backpacking equipment. New materials, new designs and new approaches have created new products and refinements of old standbys. Huge changes are taking place in the industry. To take advantage of the latest technologies in products, either on the market or in development stage, I highly recommend that potential purchasers of equipment review *Backpacker* magazine to educate themselves on any backpacking product they wish to purchase. *Backpacker's* editorial staff conducts tests of new products coming on the market and reports their results in the magazine. For the best overall view of products available, I would suggest consulting the yearly review edition (March), which contains about as complete a compilation of equipment, tester /user comments and manufacturers as is to be found anywhere in one place. This information can also be viewed online at http://www.backpacker.com.

5

Boots & Clothing

*"Any affectation whatsoever in dress implies, in
my mind, a flaw in the understanding."*
Lord Chesterfield

BOOTS

Almost everyone will agree that boots are a necessity. But even
that is open to discussion. I have met people who hiked in jogging
shoes. Eighty-four year-old Granny Gatewood thru-hiked the entire Trail end-to-end in sneakers. Trail lore relates that the sneaker
company, as part of a promotional effort, kept her resupplied when
hers wore out. I know one woman who hiked parts of the Trail in
her bare feet. Not recommended!

I personally went through four pairs of boots, although admit-
tedly they were really glorified jogging shoes. While weighing very
little, they broke down and wore out quickly. I was not very smart
about buying my boots.

Most hikers wear real hiking boots. I do too — now. Not the
heavy wafflestompers that promise to last until the next millen-
nium but lightweight boots, providing support as well as protection
and not requiring a prolonged break-in period.

Quality in a boot is important. I know from experience that it is difficult while on the Trail to find a store carrying quality hiking boots. Moreover, realize that replacing boots on the Trail will require breaking them in while hiking. This is a likelihood filled with possible disaster.

Place footgear selection in perspective. A potential thru-hiker will take about five million steps to move his body and his pack from Springer Mountain to Katahdin. These boots have to be tough, five million steps tough, an awesome figure to contemplate while shopping. But more than tough, they must also be foot-friendly. It's senseless to have rugged, high-quality hiking boots gathering dust in the corner of a shelter, while you agonize over feet in shreds from an improper fit.

Where to start in selecting boots for a thru-hike — or any hike? Considerations in buying boots fall into four major categories: price, construction, performance qualities and fit.

Price is usually an indicator of quality. But sometimes a less expensive boot of comparable quality will do the job as well as a more expensive boot. One should shop carefully and compare prices.

One manufacturer retails a line of specialized boots for as much as $450 a pair. Other companies sell lines of general hiking boots for under $100. Of course, one can also buy cheaper boots in a discount store at half the price of quality boots. But the hiker's problem is: What to do when they blow out at 6,000 feet on Clingman's Dome? Better buy quality boots that will get you to the summit of Baxter Peak. This will be money well spent. In general, expect to pay between $100 and $150, depending on brand-name, type of boot and quality. Sometimes one can get lucky and catch a sale. Still, approach with caution! This may be a closeout with odd sizes. Don't sacrifice fit for price.

There are in excess of 40 major foreign and domestic hiking boot manufacturers, most with multiple models for different purposes. There are mountaineering boots, rough trail boots, trail boots, off trail boots and double boots. All are designed with specific purposes in mind. For AT thru-hikers, the rough trail boot seems to have the best all-around characteristics for handling the Trail.

Most major sports footwear manufacturers have a line of hiking boots. These include Adidas, Reebok and Nike. Major outdoor equipment companies like Coleman and L.L.Bean also have boots. Reports indicate that the L.L.Bean GTX leather Cresta is an excellent hiking boot. Companies like Salomon, Hi-tec, Raichle, Asolo, Danner, Vasque and Rockport also produce hiking boots. With so many boots on the market, making a selection can be confusing. In addition to L.L.Bean's $169 Cresta boot, *Backpacker* magazine also reports favorably on the La Sportiva Storm GTX ($190), the Limmer Light Weight ($245), the Montrail Morain ($235), the Five Ten Mountain Master ($89), and the Vasque Sundowner Classic GTX ($175).

At your local library you can review copies of *Backpacker* magazine; they report results of testing they and others have conducted on boots and other hiking equipment. Prices, as well as strengths and weaknesses of each product, are given. It is an excellent guide for those planning to purchase boots or other equipment. Also, Appendix IV at the back of this book lists addresses and telephone numbers of major boot manufacturers.

Performance qualities — balance, support, cushioning, sole stiffness, waterproofing and weight preferences — are important considerations. Remember, these characteristics when shopping. Also, look at boot construction, stitching and the materials used — leather, Gore-Tex or other materials. Don't forget, carrying weight on your feet is just as tiring as carrying weight on your back.

Water resistance differs in every boot. No boot can remain dry in a torrent or in a stream. But some are less prone to becoming soaked while walking in wet grass. Leather uppers are usually considered the best if properly treated.

Construction of the boot is normally the key to its waterproof quality. Seams should be sealed, as should eyelets, hooks and their grommets. Less stitching overall helps, as does gusseting of the tongue.

The other side of the waterproofing scale is that under normal conditions your foot will produce about a half-pint of perspiration a day. Because my boots had no ventilation to allow moisture to evaporate, my feet were constantly wet. As a result, at the end of the day, my toes resembled large white prunes. When I hit the shelter, before doing anything else, I removed my boots and wore sandals to allow my feet to air out. Certain boots are made of material that allows perspiration to evaporate, yet remain water resistant from the outside. These are generally boots constructed with Gore-Tex or other breathable fabrics.

What type of boot is right for the AT? The guidelines for boot selection should be: (1) the rougher the trail and the heavier the load, the more support needed; (2) the bumpier and rockier the trail, the stiffer the sole. The AT is very rough, bumpy and rocky, and you will be carrying a heavy load. Judge accordingly.

Take your time in the selection. Faced with a number of styles and brands of boots, talk with the clerk about your plans and qualities you feel are important. Try on various boots and compare. Remember to take along the sock combination you plan to wear on the Trail.

Don't worry about sizes. One size-ten may be another brand's number nine or eleven. Keep trying, until the fit is right. Boots should feel snug but not tight, roomy but not loose. Keep a finger's width of room between your toes and the toe of the boot. Kick the toe of the boot against the floor. If your toes hit the boot toe, your toes will be very painful after a prolonged period hiking downhill. The heel pocket is also very important. There should be no excess movement up, down or sideways. If there is, blisters will develop. The tongue should allow the foot easy entry and removal. But it also should not contain so much material that it wrinkles and bunches at the ankle.

Lace the boot carefully, loose over the toes, snug over the instep and tighter at the ankle. Walk around to get a feel of the balance and the stiffness of the sole. Kneel and flex your knees. How does the boot heel react when you do that?

Pay attention to the cushioning property of the boot. After a day's hike in a pair of heavy, leather Austrian hiking boots, my feet were unusually sore. These boots were rugged and stiff-soled but with zero cushioning. Relief came after changing to lighter boots with jogging-shoe type cushioning. The comfort made a big difference in my outlook toward the hike.

After you have selected your boots, break them in. Lace up your boots, go into the woods and hike. Wear them around the house or on trips to town. Let them form to your feet. But begin slowly and work up gradually. Be sensitive to hot spots before blisters develop. If you sense a blister developing, cover the affected area with moleskin. Rub leather softener into the boot area causing the discomfort. Normally, fabric boots require only a short break-in period. Heavier, leather models require more time and effort. But once properly-seasoned, leather lasts the longest and generally provides the most support. They are also the heaviest. Most thru-hikers opt for an ankle high boot because of the ankle support provided. Boots higher than ankle length may rub against the shin or calf leading to discomfort. Some boots have a notch in the heel. This prevents the boot top from irritating or pressing against the wearer's Achilles tendon. If you have tender or sensitive Achilles tendons, perhaps you should look at this type of boot. After prolonged use, your boots will fit differently than when they were new. Expect this to happen. They will widen at the ball of the foot, the ankle will crinkle down, and the boot's interior will stretch. An extra pair of socks or adhesive-backed felt pads may help the boot feel a little tighter.

Socks can be as important to foot comfort as boots. A sock that bunches up can cause blistering. Socks that fit well complement the boot and add to comfort. Normally, thru-hikers should wear two pairs of socks. A lightweight, tight-fitting polypro or polyester sock should be worn against the skin. A thicker, cushion sole or padded sock is worn over the first sock. The two socks slide against one another, thereby reducing the skin friction that causes blisters.

Wool is a good material for an outer sock. It stays warm when wet, and the fabric does not compress as readily as other fabrics. However, it chafes easily and is usually combined with nylon or other strengthening material to reduce chafing susceptibility.

Considerable debate has arisen among the environmentally conscious about the impact on the environment of lug-sole boots. Detractors claim it causes trail erosion, particularly during spring when trails are wet. They recommend wearing light weight boots with smoother soles to preclude erosion damage. Others say that any traffic on wet trails is going to have an impact and that the safety provided by lug-soles is more important. I prefer the lug-sole for extra traction in slippery conditions and light boots; I am into paring weight!

CLOTHING

Most material I studied in preparation for hiking the AT recommended wearing long trousers to protect the legs. Imagine my surprise to discover I was the only thru-hiker wearing long pants.

During summer in the southern Appalachians, most people wear jogging shorts; they are cooler, lighter, and easier to clean. However, I continued with my long pants; they had deep pockets (invaluable for carrying *Trail Guides* and maps) and dried quickly when wet. I would do it again. But that's a very personal preference of a hiker's choice in clothing.

Actually, clothing selection for a thru-hike is fairly simple: cool when it's hot, warm when it's cold, dry when it's wet, weigh nothing and easy-to-clean. And items must withstand being worn every day for six months.

Normally, people on a two-week vacation, carrying enough clothes to insure comfort under conditions described above, would fill two steamer trunks. But you have only a backpack, and your whole house is already in it.

A relevant fact in planning your clothing needs is temperature. At 7:00 a.m. on Springer Mountain or any other mountain in March or April, it is often below freezing. By 1:00 p.m., it can be hot. At 5:00 p.m., it is cold again. Even in July, temperature ranges can be extreme, especially in the northern mountains of Vermont, New Hampshire and Maine. In the southern Appalachians in the summer, it may be very hot all the time. In addition to the outside temperatures, hikers perspire profusely from exertion, and the evaporation of moisture can affect body temperature. Thru-hikers must understand the impact of temperature and be prepared to handle the extremes. What to do? For cold weather, carry sufficient clothing to dress in layers. The layer system has three components, the under layer, a second insulation layer and a third outer layer or shell.

During periods of extremely cold weather, hikers should wear, as an under layer, a long sleeve top of polypro or polyester and long-johns of the same material. The top should be equipped with a zip T-neck seal and long-johns should be snug to the ankle to maintain body warmth. Both polypro and polyester have spectacular water-repellent characteristics. These reduce the threat of excessive body cooling through evaporation and the resulting dangers of hypothermia.

The second layer should consist of a medium weight wool or fleece sweater. This creates dead air space and traps body heat. Other insulating wear includes down or fleece vests which can be difficult to maintain. Down, after repeated use and compacting, has a tendency to lose its puffiness, and when wet it is useless.

The third layer, to protect against wind, rain or snow, should generally not be insulated. The shell should be long enough that it doesn't lump up under your pack. You might take your pack along when you buy this item. It should also have pockets for accessible storage of items like *Trail Guides* and maps.

Various fabrics are used in outer layer material. Some are highly wind-resistant but barely water-resistant. Others are water-resistant only if they are separately waterproofed. The best are waterproof, breathable and wind-resistant.

Waterproof and breathable means the material allows perspiration to ventilate but keeps moisture (rain or snow) outside. Gore-Tex or Sympatex are two of the most popular waterproof/breathable materials. Purely waterproof material that is non-breathable is effective against rain and snow but does not allow water to vent to the outside. As a result, you become as drenched inside the shell as you would be outside the shell. This can be a serious problem for hikers who perspire freely. I learned that one the hard way too. I solved it with a the purchase of a Gore-Tex jacket. During the day, as the temperature builds, take time to remove the outer layers. Conversely, as evening approaches and temperatures decrease replace the layers.

During hot weather, wear a cotton T-shirt and loose fitting shorts. Cotton absorbs moisture and dries slowly which aids in evaporative cooling for the body.

If you are concerned about skin rashes, insect bites or cuts on your legs while passing through briars or blackberry bushes, I suggest long pants. However, as I indicated above, most everyone hikes in shorts, and none seemed to notice the inevitable minor scrapes and scratches.

I carried two brown cotton t-shirts, one lightweight long sleeve cotton poplin shirt, four underpants, four pairs of socks, one pair of shorts with pockets, a medium sweater, a Gore-tex jacket, two bandanas, two small handkerchiefs and a wide brimmed tennis hat. This was sufficient, except in New Hampshire, where I bought a pair of woolen gloves. I washed my clothes often. This wardrobe was fully adequate for hiking in the temperate climate during spring, summer and fall.

6

Packs & Bedding

"Now hollow fires burn out to black,
And lights are guttering low:
"Square your shoulders, lift your pack
And leave your friends and go."
A. E. Housman

PACKS

A light, durable, well-fitting backpack is the most efficient way to transport a thru-hiker's backwoods household. The pack must carry everything needed for survival on the Trail and be reasonably "comfortable" to wear. Or if not "comfortable," it should at least not cause totally debilitating pain.

"Comfort," when used to describe a backpack, is a relative term. Actually, a "comfortable pack" is an oxymoron. Strapping fifty pounds on one's back to walk 2,000 miles in the mountains can be described by many terms, but "comfortable" is not one of them. More likely, one will experience pain, certainly during the first few days. After that, the experience is one of discomfort more than pain. As the body and muscles toughen and become accustomed to the pack weight, the shoulder harness and waist belt, the discomfort eventually becomes unnoticeable. That is when the pack becomes "comfortable."

If a pack has been properly fitted and the load balanced, the pain or discomfort period is quickly reduced. If not properly fitted or balanced, the pain can lead to hiker exhaustion, and if not corrected, may over time result in injury. Succinctly said: A quality pack, properly fitted and balanced, usually means the difference between an enjoyable hike and a miserable one.

Use the advice of others as a starting point when choosing a pack, but do not let them unduly influence your selection. Personal satisfaction is of paramount importance. After a few weeks on the Trail, your pack becomes almost a part of your body. That means it must conform to your body as individually as your boots do to your feet. Only you can make those decisions.

You should list all the attributes and features you desire in your pack and then start the process of selection. Essential steps and considerations in this process should include:

- First, measure your torso so you can establish a pack size.
- Take your time in making a decision.
- Know how much of a load you will be carrying to be sure your pack will accommodate it all. Pack capacity ranges from 2,500 cubic inches, for small day treks, to 6,000 cubic inches, for those out for the long haul.
- Consider the trails you will be hiking. Are they well maintained, or are they rough rising-and-descending rock pathways filled with roots and rocks? This is important from a stability standpoint. External frames work well on cleared and maintained trails. For rough-and-rocky walking, the internal frame provides more stability (no open frame parts to catch branches).
- Consider ease of drinking. Many packs now come equipped with water bladder compartments with hydration tubes so you can drink while on the move. This saves the considerable energy you would expend removing and then replacing the pack, just to take a drink. Some packs also come with deep pockets designed to hold water bottles.

One should also determine whether panel loading or top loading is preferable. For those who desire an organized pack, panel loading might be attractive. The entire front of the pack opens and displays everything inside. Top loaders load everything from the top. Hybrids have both, a top loading compartment and a panel loading section beneath. Some packs come with a floating top pocket, which is convenient for storing often-used items or last-minute additions. Also useful are compression straps, which support zippered areas.

As with other equipment, pack manufacturers have introduced specialization. There are now packs for almost every hiking purpose and region of the world. For the prospective AT thru-hiker, the choice is simple: to carry as efficiently, and as comfortably as possible, the equipment one needs to reach the summit of Katahdin or Springer Mountain. All else is window dressing.

For the AT thru-hiker's purpose, the first decision is whether to get an internal frame or an external frame pack. Significant differences exist between these two types. First, there is the frame itself. The external is basically an aluminum or composite material frame with a harness attached to one side and an equipment bag to the other. The harness is worn by the hiker, and the bag is filled with equipment and supplies.

The internal frame pack means exactly that — a pack with its frame internal. The frame is simple, usually two flattened curved stays. Sometimes they are crossed, sometimes parallel. The carrying harness is attached directly to the pack itself.

Early in my hike, I replaced my internal frame pack with an external frame pack — a big improvement. My external frame allowed cooling air to circulate between the cargo sack and my back. That can be important in July in Virginia. Its disadvantage is the tendency to ride high on the wearer's back. The frame catches low-hanging tree and mountain laurel branches, especially if the hiker is tall. Also, if not properly loaded, it has a tendency to pull backward at the shoulder and push forward on the wearer's hips. The internal frame will do that too but not to such a degree; its center of gravity is lower. Also, the internal frame, molded to the wearer's body, does not catch low hanging branches so easily. Internal frame packs have more appeal to those who hike at higher elevations or hike cross-country away from trails. External frame packs appeal to those who hike in hot weather and on established trails.

Most external frames have multiple outside pockets sewn directly on the cargo sack; this allows for separating items and retrieving them quickly when needed. For example, toilet paper, matches and first aid kit in one pocket, stove and fuel in another pocket, cookpot and canteen in another.

Many internal frames have only the large cavity into which everything is stuffed — very inconvenient for locating often-used items. Recently, however, some manufacturers have begun fitting internal frames packs with external pockets. Some even have detachable pockets. A great idea!

After selecting the type of pack, the fit is crucial. With the external frame, size is most important. It must fit your torso and should not flop around on your back. Shoulder straps should allow room for adjustment. The hip belt should fit around the waist with some material to spare.

To test the pack, fill it with the weight you plan to carry, then put it on. Adjust the yoke or the hip belt or both, according to the instructions that come with the pack. Get a salesman or an experienced hiker to help. Cinch up the hip belt as tightly as possible until the weight rides on your hips. Adjust the yoke so that your shoulders carry a minimum of weight. Then, walk around and, if possible, take a "test drive."

Fitting an internal frame is more demanding than fitting an external frame. First, pack size must correspond to your body measurements. Referring to manufacturer's size instructions should help. Remove the stays and shape them to the contour of your back. This will require time and patience. Measure the distance between the base of your spine and the point where your shoulders meet your neck and adjust the pack harness so that the bottom of the lumbar pad is the same distance from the arch of the shoulder straps. Don your pack and insure that the torso length is correct by checking then adjusting the shoulder harness lift straps. You will probably have to experiment before you get it right. Next, determine how you want to load your pack. This makes a difference in comfort and efficiency. The objective is to adhere as closely as possible to the wearer's center of gravity. Actually, there is considerable debate about the wisdom of maintaining a high center of gravity. To achieve high centers of gravity, load lighter weight items in the bottom and heavier items at the top. Heavy items should be positioned as close to the wearer's back as possible. Women, who have lower centers of gravity than men, should adhere to a lower center of gravity for their packs.

Determining your proper center of gravity is a personal choice. You can do everything exactly by the book and still have an uncomfortable load. Body conformation and center of gravity are very personal. By experimenting, you can determine what is right for you. Load your pack and start walking. After a while, rearrange your load and walk some more. Somewhere down the trail, maybe on the Appalachian Trail, you will find the right combination. You will know when it's right.

Quality of construction is important in pack selection. Double stitching of seams and zippers makes a difference in durability. In zipper material, look for nylon which does not corrode and tends to function more smoothly than metal. Pay attention to frame construction on external frame packs and the hardware used to attach the harness and cargo sack to the frame. Welded aluminium frames have a good reliability record. Also, look at fasteners holding the hardware together. Screws and nuts have a tendency to work loose, and replacements may be a problem. Metal rods and pins with split rings are usually pretty reliable but are more likely to catch on branches or brush. In any case, carry spares of your pack's hardware.

Pack manufacturers offer a variety of models and prices. Good equipment is not cheap; expect to pay between $150 and $300 for a pack. Leading pack makers include Kelty, JanSport, Camp Trails, REI, The North Face and Sierra Designs. Kelty packs seemed to be popular during my hikes. Appendix IV lists the major pack manufacturers, their addresses, telephone numbers and website addresses.

SLEEPING BAGS

Most people assume that sleeping bags only keep the cold out. The real purpose of the bag is to maintain a balance between the heat you generate inside the bag and the heat lost through the bag to the outside. If the bag simply maintained heat and allowed none to escape, it would soon become unbearably hot.

The sleeping bag maintains body heat through the fill, which holds the pockets of air that provide insulation. The fewer the pockets of air, the less the insulation. Conversely, the more air pockets, the more insulation. The most efficient fill, goose down, creates the most air pockets. It is also the most expensive fill. Down also retains its loft, or height, longer than synthetic fill. Down does not dry easily when wet, however, and it loses its insulating capacity.

The least expensive fill is synthetic. Although not as efficient as down, synthetic fill is getting close. Some synthetic fills in use at the time of this printing include DuPont's Thermolite (Extreme, Extra, Micro, Plus, Active, Microloft) and Hollofil (II and 808) and Quallofil (with or without Allerban, an antimicrobial), Albany International Corp.'s Primaloft (PL1, PL2 and PL Lite), 3M's Thinsulate (Regular, Flex, Lite Loft, Ultra and Extreme), and The Lessinger Group's Polarguard (Classic, HV, Delta and 3D). You can keep up with improvements in these companies' fiber insulation technologies by regularly visiting their websites: DuPont (http://www.dupont.com), Albany International Corp. (http://www.albint.com), The Lessinger Group (http://www.polarguard.com) and 3M (http://www.3M.com/thinsulate).

The outside of the bag, the shell, is simply the covering or protection for the fill. It maintains bag shape, keeps fill in place and distributed throughout the bag, and protects against water and dirt. Shells can be made from nylon, polyester, ripstop fabric (nylon or polyester with a heavy thread running through it, often in a diamond shape, to prevent or minimize ripping), taffeta, cotton, canvas, and other, more high-tech fabrics.

Nylon, polyester and taffeta are the least-durable materials; however, they offer low cost and breathable comfort for cool to hot camping in dry weather. They are available in a variety of weave tightnesses; the tighter the weave, the more wind and water resistant the fabric. Ripstop fabrics are more durable, and they offer more moisture resistance than plain nylon or polyester fabrics or taffeta. Canvas and cotton shells are inexpensive, but they do not repel water well, can be heavy and are even heavier when wet. Canvas and cotton shells may be good choices for dry, mild-climate, short-term camping.

High-tech shell materials are probably the best bet for cold weather camping, especially when a threat of rain or snow exists. However, with increased waterproofing, fabrics lose some breathability. W. L. Gore & Associates makes Gore-Tex fabrics (2-layer, 3-layer, Paclite, Supprescent, Immersion, Coastal, Ocean) and DryLoft, a highly recommended Gore-Tex alternative that allows more breathability than traditional Gore-Tex. Gore-Tex is an excellent choice when looking at an overbag or bivy sack to supplement your sleeping bag for winter camping or camping in extreme conditions.

DryLoft is the premium choice for shells. It's ideal for four-season camping, canoe camping, or extended stays in the backcountry. SympaTex Technologies makes SympaTex, a fabric popular in Europe for bivy sacs. To keep up with new shell technologies, regularly visit the high-tech fabric-makers' websites: W. L. Gore & Associates (http://www.gore.com/corp/fabrics) and SympaTex (http://www.sympatex.com).

Sleeping bags come in two styles, mummys and rectangulars. In the mummy bag, the head is enclosed and the draw strings can be tightened to restrict loss of heat. The rectangular bags are like blankets where heat can escape through the top of the bag around the head and shoulders.

The average AT thru-hiker will be sleeping in temperatures well below freezing in the mountains in late March and early April. During July and August the weather will be very warm, often in the 70s and 80s, even at high elevation. This range of temperatures makes bag selection difficult.

Most thru-hikers will probably want a three-season bag. It will be comfortable when temperatures are below freezing. When it becomes too hot, the bag can be opened up to allow excess heat to escape. If the bag is too light, it will be impossible to generate enough heat to be comfortable during lower temperature periods.

Bags come in different sizes and lengths. Decide which size is best for you by actually getting into the bag. It should not unduly restrict movement. Consider additional room to keep clothes or other equipment in the bag with you. You should be able to turn and move inside the bag but not get lost in the folds. Too much airspace inside the bag defeats its temperature-balancing property.

Sleeping bags come in a wide range of prices, depending on quality and purpose. Top-quality, custom-made mummy bags sell for as high as $600. Normally, they cost between $120 and $175. Your bag will have to work for 2,000 miles; it is best to pay the price and get the durability. All the major outdoor sports equipment makers include sleeping bags in their line of products.

The stuff sacks sold with sleeping bags are notoriously small. A larger stuff sack will reduce the amount of compression in the fill. When storing the bag for any length of time, remove it from the stuff sack. Lay it out or hang it up, so that the fill remains expanded.

MATTRESSES

Basically, mattresses are either sleeping pads or air mattresses. Pads are either closed-cell foam or open-cell foam. Closed-cell foam is basically indestructible, densely packed, tiny plastic bubbles formed into sheets of varying thickness. Closed-cell foam is quite rigid but provides good insulation. Open-cell foam is much softer and spongy but tends to suck up moisture. Having used both, I found that neither were sufficient by themselves. The closed-cell sleeping pad was too hard; the open-cell foam pad became wet too easily. The air mattresses lost air.

Fortunately, several companies now offer a closed-cell/open-cell hybrid pad. By bonding a layer of closed-cell foam to a layer of open-cell foam, and encasing the result in a water- and tear-resistant cover, they combine the advantages of a durable insulation base with a soft, comfortable top panel. Other innovations to pads include webbing straps and buckles, which allow the pad to convert to a camp chair. Roll straps help compress the pad into a smaller roll. Some pads even include chambers that can be adjusted to cushion different parts of the body, and others are available in mummy shapes to conform to the body. Non-slip surfaces help keep pads from sliding on the ground, which is a benefit for the toss-and-turn sleeper.

Mattress and pad sizes range in length from around 72 inches for full sizes to 42 inches for hip-length models in widths of 20 to 28 inches. Since air mattresses in general and the Therm-A-Rest in particular tend to be on the slippery side, Cascade Designs has invented a non-sticky aerosol spray that works well in keeping sleeping bags from sliding off mattresses. Another variation is to glue strips of Velcro pile across the mattress.

PILLOWS

Some people sleep with large pillows, others with small pillows and some with no pillows at all. In the backwoods, those who sleep with no pillows are in luck. Those who like small pillows are only slightly challenged, but those who love big feather pillows may encounter problems. I like big pillows but learned to survive by rolling my trousers, a sweater and windbreaker together, and placing them into a stuff sack. Decent — but not luxurious sleeping!

7

Tents & Bivouac Sacks

"'Tis ever common
That men are merriest when they are from home."
Shakespeare

TENTS

Although I met several thru-hikers who carried no tent, I highly recommend beginning with some type of portable shelter. This provides flexibility in responding to unforeseen circumstances. The AT has many shelters, and after 10 hours of hill climbing, some can seem like castles. However, they *all* have become home to many critters, ground squirrels and mice, in particular.

For some, the convenience of the shelter may pale in comparison to the constant patter and rustle in the darkness as mice scamper around the shelter and over equipment. Those squeamish about sleeping with mice may find sleeping in a tent an attractive alternative.

Insects can present another problem at shelters, particularly, mosquitoes and no-see-ums as well as honey bees and yellow jackets. In North Georgia, I was driven from a shelter by honey bees. They weren't angry or upset, they just swarmed all over me and my equipment. I thought it provident to depart. Tents DO keep insects out!

Also, occasionally, shelters will be filled with other hikers.

Or, you may find a Boy Scout troop has taken over a shelter at which you planned to stay. Sleeping is very difficult when surrounded by twenty keyed-up adolescents. Sometimes, shelters are located near roads. This provides attractive places for locals to party. Sometimes, shelters are "appropriated" by derelicts or campers spending a couple of weeks in the woods.

At those times, continue down the Trail to the next shelter. But, what if the next shelter is 10 miles away and it is already 6 P.M.? The answer is your tent or your bivy.

Tent selection requires study. It entails product knowledge, detailed usage knowledge, and patience. Two qualities, weight and space, rule the selection process. No two shelters strike the same balance, so you will have to prioritize your requirements and factor in the features you desire. Some of the features and checks you may want to consider, including weight and spatial desires, are:

- Ease in set-up and take-down. Practice pitching the tent in the store. Imagine doing it in wind and rain.
- Check the rainfly fit. The panels need to be taut so they don't flap or act like sails in the wind. Be sure the rainfly reaches to the ground.
- Hold fabric against the light to check seams and material for flaws. Carefully check the inside seam stitching and the fabric for irregularities and discoloration.
- Look for potential leak causers like wrinkles under seams. Scratch seams and tape to see if they separate.
- Test critical components. Tug on guy posts, stake webbing, and pole attachment points to see if seams start to separate. Insure guy pole grommets are secure and that there is not excessive tension on zippers.
- Tent coating should appear as a shiny, waterproof coating on the inside of the rainfly and floor. If you can't see or feel waterproofing, it may not be durable for heavy use.
- Check the color. Light colors create a brighter interior, darker colors absorb solar energy in cold weather.
- Consider a tent with a vestibule to protect the entrance.

One and two man tents weigh between two and six pounds. Bivys weigh between a pound and a quarter and two pounds. Specialization is in! There are tents for summer, tents for three seasons, excluding snow, tents for all the seasons and tents for the mountains.

Most thru-hikers hike in spring, summer and fall. Obviously, the three season tent best fills their needs. These are constructed in two parts, a breathable fabric inner tent and a waterproof outer fly. The working premise is that the occupant's body heat will cause interior moisture to push through the inner tent, while the tent fly keeps rain outside.

Another design uses a single, breathable, waterproof fabric like Gore-Tex to do the same thing. Whatever the material and however constructed, when the inside of the tent becomes warmer than the outside of the tent, condensation forms on the inside. This problem can be controlled by insect-proof, screened vents woven into the top of the tent allowing air to circulate and moisture to evaporate.

Different tent shapes have different characteristics. Dome tents and hoop or tunnel tents offer the most interior space. A disadvantage of dome tents is their relatively high vertical profile makes them susceptible to the effects of high winds. A-frame tents are less likely to be affected by wind, but provide less interior head space. Free standing tents, the easiest to erect and clean, are widely available. All types of tents need some type of anchoring. Free-standing tents are no exception and can be temporarily anchored with three or four stakes. Other tents, particularly A-frame tents require more stakes, sometimes many more.

Poles, guy-lines and stakes all add weight. Aluminum poles are the lightest but also the most expensive and represent a major part of the cost in some tents. Fiber glass poles are a little heavier, but less expensive. They are not as sturdy as aluminum poles and those assembled in shock cord sections develop cracks along the ferrules if handled roughly. Carbon fiber is a fairly new tent pole or frame material, but it is expensive. All in all, aluminum has the best weight-to-strength ratio.

Deciding how big a tent to buy depends on how many hikers and how much gear will be in the tent. If you hike solo, it's just you and your pack, assuming you want your pack in the tent. Many hikers don't. I didn't. I brought only my sleeping gear and clothes inside my tent. Some folks like to cook in their tents. I felt it was too hazardous to cook in my tent so I bought a tent with a vestibule. That way I could cook "outside" and still be protected from the rain.

If you plan to bring your pack into the tent with you, look for a two-man tent. Allow twelve square feet per person when calculating tentage requirements. Add at least another six feet for equipment. As you calculate space, remember, the larger the tent, the more it weighs.

To prepare the tent for use and reduce leaks, seal the floor and seams with tent sealer. Carry sealer in your miscellaneous kit or send some in a mail drop for later use. I sealed my tent a second time in Vermont after it began leaking. This makes a big difference in keeping a sleeping bag dry. Seal both sides of floor seams and reinforcement areas such as pole tabs and corners.

To keep from having to dig through your pack every time you erect your tent, keep guy-lines and stakes in the stuff bag with the tent. Stuff bags that come with tents are usually totally unrelated to the size of the tent. Often it is impossible to get the tent and stakes in the same bag. In fact, when the tent is wet it is impossible to get it alone into the bag. Solution: buy a bigger stuff sack.

Stuff the tent into the stuff sack, as the name implies. Don't roll or fold it. The idea is to avoid creasing the material. In the event it is wet and you are heading home — dry out the tent before storing it. If stored wet, the tent will likely become a mildewed mess.

Pitch your tent well off and out of sight of the Trail. It should be protected from wind and located well away from streams or lakes. The ground should be level, or nearly level, free from roots and rocks and not cover the entrance to the homes of forest critters: snakes, squirrels, ants or burrowing animals. Carry a ground cloth, a lightweight nylon or polyethylene sheet, to reduce wear from rocks and rough ground on the floor of your tent.

Remove your boots before entering the tent. Grinding mud or sand into the tent floor will quickly damage it. To clean a tent, simply turn it inside out and shake it. That clears the leaves and associated dirt that find their way into the tents of even the most fastidious hikers. Carry a small broom, if you feel it necessary.

For those seeking a lighter way to go, a "pyramid" tent may be the answer. This is as light as some bivys (two and a half pounds with poles, pegs and stuff sack), but much roomier, four people roomier. The "pyramid" is basically a rainfly with a center pole. The corners and sides of the "pyramid" are anchored by stakes. While it won't keep out animals or insects, it does protect from rain and will deflect wind if pitched low enough to the ground.

Bivys are the smallest and lightest of all. Basically enlarged sleeping bag shells, they are separated from you and your sleeping bag by a couple of small hoops. These do keep you dry in rain and keep out unwanted visitors. From a roominess standpoint, they are quite restrictive. If you are claustrophobic, look for a tent.

STOVES

A stove's only purpose is to heat your food. Once I did start a fire in a rain storm with wet wood by using my Whisperlite stove as a fire starter. So my first statement is only 99.99 percent accurate.

Many potential hikers view the ultimate wilderness experience as sitting around a campfire cowboy-style eating stew and drinking black coffee from tin cups. Wrong!

It is often difficult to find suitable wood for campfires around shelters on the AT. The surrounding woods have been picked clean long before you arrived. Also, cooking over an open wood fire can be difficult, as well as time consuming for the inexperienced. First, one has to find the wood, haul it to the fire site, cut it, build or clear a fire pit and start the fire. Not always easy, especially if you have just finished humping 50 pounds for 10 hours. Then, you must constantly tend the fire and the meal, and, often as not, half of it ends up spilled in the fire.

Easier, cleaner, faster, environmentally friendlier and safer is the pack stove. I could start my stove, begin cooking dinner and continue setting up camp or writing in my journal while the food cooked.

When shopping for a stove, look for: weight, ease of setup, ease of lighting, stability, reliability, power, maintenance and price.

Stove weights minus fuel generally run between ten ounces and one pound, ten ounces. Fuel tanks and fuel add another pound to a pound and a half, lighter than carrying a hatchet.

Setup involves assembling the stove and filling the fuel tank, sometimes difficult in cold weather with cold fingers.

Stability involves keeping the stove upright under a full pot of water under field conditions like sloping ground and slippery tent vestibules.

Power means how much heat it produces measured by how quickly it brings one quart of water to a boil. This indicates how rapidly it will cook your meal.

A reliable stove will operate at any time, all the time, whenever the need arises without requiring the user to have an engineering degree. It also means it can be carried and handled easily, be easy to clean and keep in operating order.

The main differences in stoves is in the fuel used. Some models, multifuel stoves, burn everything from auto gas to kerosene. Some stoves burn only specific fuels.

White gas seems the most efficient and maintenance-free fuel, and it is widely available. Butane is as efficient as white gas, but it is more expensive, is contained in metal cartridges, and it is not always available on the Trail. Regular auto gas is sooty and not recommended! Alcohol stoves, while "environmentally correct," are only about half as efficient as ones with similar amounts of white gas and butane.

A number of other fuels are available, such as isobutane, isopropane and blended fuel canisters. Butane burns cooler and produces a smaller flame but burns to the last drop. Isopropane burns hotter and also burns completely. Blended fuel canisters contain a blend of propane and butane and sometimes isobutane and isopropane, which improves steadier heat output until the canister is completely empty.

Another stove recently on the market is a natural fuel stove called "Zip Ztove." It produces heat equal to white gas by use of a small C-battery powered fan that pushes air into the fire chamber, acting like a bellows. Fuel can be twigs, pine cones, grass, leaves or whatever is available. It comes with its own one-quart cookpot. Detractors say it burns wet wood poorly and is unstable. Its obvious advantage is weight; the user carries no fuel. The disadvantages appear to be unreliability and instability.

Take your new stove into the field and give it a "test drive." Pack the stove separately from cooking utensils. Avoid overheating the fuel tank. Light the stove away from your face to avoid injury in case of a flare-up. Many stoves come with metal windscreens which not only protect from wind, but contain the heat under the cookpot. These can reduce fuel consumption by up to 50 percent.

Do not cook too close to a sleeping bag. The shell of the bag is usually nylon which melts easily. Carry a stove repair kit: needle to clean jets, a wrench (one normally comes with the stove) and pump washers.

Appendix IV contains a list of stove manufacturers.

8

Other Equipment

"Man is a tool using animal . . .
without tools he is nothing,
with tools he is all."
Thomas Carlyle

Sometimes equipment or supplies carried by hikers seem irrelevant to need. Or if related to need, it is only in the sense that the hiker has become accustomed to certain modern conveniences. This is evidenced by the enormity of the packs strapped to some people's backs.

People are willing to carry the strangest things into the wilderness. One man reportedly had a portable TV in his tent. Another was sighted with a metal and canvas camp stool dangling from his pack. Another carried a golfing umbrella.

I doubt a thru-hiker would dig a portable TV from his pack. That would border on sacrilegious. However, backpackers are an independent breed. What they carry is limited only by bulk, weight and their imaginations.

Some do carry equipment for special purposes. Dan "Wingfoot" Bruce, a seven-time end-to-end thru-hiker, carried a TV camera as part of a promotional effort in 1987 during his 50th AT Anniversary Commemorative Hike. Others have also carried TV cameras to record their adventures. Marvelous (and profitable) pictorial histories have resulted.

Some now carry cellular phones as part of their basic equipment. Not a bad idea for emergency situations but certainly not an "essential" piece of equipment. Some mention has been made of hand-held Global Positioning System (GPS) computers (devices that rely on satellite signals to determine their position on the earth). If one is carrying a topographic map, location can be pinpointed to within a few meters. Such instruments are enormously valuable for navigation at sea, or in trackless deserts or jungles where identifiable terrain features are nonexistent. But on the AT, which is clearly blazed, such instruments are irrelevant.

However, most hikers carry the equipment items listed below. (While not everyone carried all these items, a sufficient number did. Therefore, these items should be considered.)

KNIVES

Forget the eight-inch "Bowie Knives" carried by bear hunters to skin game or hurl at adversaries. These are too heavy, too cumbersome and too one-dimensional for use in a thru-hiking role. Concentrate instead on finding a pocketknife with a combination of tools useful in a variety of situations.

The most widely known is probably the Swiss Army Knife. This comes in at least a dozen models with various combinations of scissors, can openers, cork screws, tweezers, toothpicks, awls, saw blades, fish scalers, flat screw drivers, Phillip's head screwdrivers, file blades and one or two knife blades. Some even have spoons and forks. Those with all the "bells and whistles" can be up to three inches wide and six inches long, and cost upwards of $100. For the Trail, that is overkill.

A pocketknife with a three or four-inch blade, can opener, scissors, corkscrew, and screwdriver/bottle opener-combination provides all the tools a thru-hiker really needs. At least, this provided everything I needed. I expected to use the knife portion and the can opener frequently but was surprised how often the scissors proved useful.

Another highly regarded knife, the SwissBuck, is made by Buck Knives, Inc., a firm with a reputation for quality. Like the

Swiss Army Knife, SwissBuck comes in a variety of models offering various combinations of tools. The Swiss Advantage model incorporates scissors, screwdriver, nail file, corkscrew, awl, can opener and, of course, a regular blade. It costs about $40. Prices for similar models vary from store-to-store, so shop around.

Several other pocketknives are available, some with the same tools listed above. Metal quality is extremely important, and the Swiss Army Knife and the SwissBuck are noted for their quality.

FLASHLIGHTS

Almost everyone on the Trail carries a flashlight. It is extremely valuable when it becomes necessary to relieve yourself in the middle of the night or to make a shelter after sundown. Some hikers wear miners' type headlamps for hiking at night. (I don't recommend that. Part of the AT experience is observing nature and the scenery through which the Trail passes; and night hiking limits that.)

Any outdoor equipment store carries a variety of flashlights. Some are very good. Others are mediocre or less. When shopping for flashlights keep in mind its purpose. It doesn't need to cast a 500,000 candle power halogen beam a half mile. But it should be able to illuminate the pathway and direct a beam of light for a few yards. It should be light, reliable, easy-to-use and not burn batteries by the case. It should also be capable of being rigged to hold between your teeth or attached to a headband to free your hands for other work.

Perhaps the most popular flashlight on the Trail is the MiniMagLite. It produces exceptional light with very little weight. It takes two AA batteries which, for my purposes, lasted the entire 2,100 miles. A very appealing feature of this light is that it is activated by twisting the head of the lamp, and by twisting the head, one can narrow or diffuse the focus of the light. Most equipment stores carry headband devices, or ones that allow the user to hold the light between the teeth. The MiniMagLite is expensive in comparison to other lights — around $15.

The plastic Mallory is a rugged and highly regarded flashlight that comes in two models, using AA batteries and costing only about $3; it's a favorite among backpackers, since it is inexpensive, and its rectangular body is easy to hold between the teeth.

Another product recently on the market is the Durabeam Compact by Duracell. It weighs three ounces and sells for $4.

Other makes and models abound. You can spend much time testing and comparing. Be careful of lights with button switches. These are notoriously unreliable, because they can easily be turned on accidentally.

PACK COVERS

New packs, depending on their material, are normally quite water-resistant. However, with rough use and even limited aging, the best material quickly loses its water repellant capability. In a downpour, all packs are vulnerable to becoming thoroughly soaked, particularly through seams and zippers. Also, tents and sleeping bags, items often tied to the outside of the pack, are particularly vulnerable. (Many hikers wrap their sleeping bags in heavy duty plastic bags that help keep them dry. However, water has an uncanny knack of finding its way into even a plastic-wrapped sleeping bag.)

The best method of protecting a pack under really bad conditions is with a pack cover. These come in a variety of sizes and shapes, and are usually made from waterproof nylon. Many models have elastic drawstrings that allow the cover to enclose the entire pack. Other covers encase the top and sides of the pack, but the bottom remains open.

I have used both types. While the cover style with the elastic draw strings encased the entire pack, water was able to penetrate the cover through the space between my back and the pack frame. Eventually, this water collected in the bottom of the cover and items in the bottom of my pack became wet. During periods of prolonged rain, this necessitated periodically removing the pack cover and emptying the accumulation of water.

The cover with the open bottom, which I suspected would be less efficient than the draw string type, proved surprisingly effective. It was made of a sturdier, rubberized material that completely covered the top and sides of the pack, and the rain that managed to get between my back and the pack frame simply dripped to the ground; the bottom of my pack remained as dry as the top.

Plan to spend about $15 for a pack cover. A cheaper alternative to a commercially sold pack cover is a large, heavy duty, plastic garbage bag that is cut to size and slipped over the pack. However, these do not have the strength of waterproof nylon and are susceptible to tears from sticks and branches.

There is nothing more miserable in a backpacker's life than opening his pack at day's end to find a wet sleeping bag, wet clothing, mushy food and soggy toilet paper. Pay the extra money; insure comfort and peace of mind.

ROPE

Supple, light, braided, nylon cord can be used for a number of purposes. My cord was about 20-feet long. I also carried several shorter pieces for general use like keeping a poncho rolled.

Mostly, I used my cord to hang my food sack from the shelter roof beams. Discs made from can or jar tops attached to the cord halfway between the pack and the ceiling proved an effective barrier to mice. Removing the food sack keeps mice from gnawing through pack fabric in search of food. Be sure to leave pack pockets open. Mice will soon learn that the pack contains no food and will look elsewhere.

When tenting I used the rope to hang my pack from tree branches, keeping it out of the reach of marauding raccoons or bears.

Occasionally, it served as a clothesline.

LANTERNS

The size and fuel requirements of kerosene lanterns makes them impractical for backpacking; however, some type of lantern can be very helpful during the night when you are looking for something inside your tent or pack or for reading. The best solution? The candle lantern. Being encased in a glass and metal enclosure provides several advantages. Foremost, it is much safer than an open candle in a shelter or a tent. An open candle is more susceptible to being knocked over and causing a fire, or spilling candle wax on the tent floor or your equipment. Another advantage is that lanterns are sturdy and most weigh only a few ounces. Kamp-Zeek, about $15, appears to be one of the best models. Limelight is also highly rated. Alpine and a folding lantern are less highly regarded.

Stearene candles are best for candle lanterns; they are inexpensive, burn slowly and drip much less than ordinary household candles.

CAMERAS

Many thru-hikers carry cameras to record special events or to capture the magnificent scenery the Trail offers. However, unless one is a professional photographer or is on a photographic safari, there is no need to carry bags of sophisticated equipment. Small, relatively simple cameras are adequate for most thru-hikers' purposes. In fact, most are likely to take better pictures with simple cameras; sophisticated equipment is too complex and time-consuming to take advantage of fleeting opportunities. Also, sophisticated equipment may not withstand the rough use on the Trail.

Wide angle lens cameras take excellent panoramic shots that allow the hiker to capture on film some of the spectacular vistas and scenery encountered on the Trail. Beyond the wide angle opportunities, occasionally one may want to take a close-up. Your camera should have both capabilities.

Canon, Olympus, Pentax, Nikon w/panoramic capability and Minox are some of the better known brands that make simple autofocus and autoshutter speed cameras. Your photos will provide many enjoyable hours as you revisit places of great beauty. If you are unfamiliar with cameras, take the time to educate yourself. Visit a professional photographer and get advice about equipment. Most camera stores can also educate you.

HIKING STICKS

Some people carry them and some don't. I carried mine for 2,100 miles and felt naked without it. It was especially useful in helping maintain balance while crossing streams or on puncheon bridges. Also, it provided support for negotiating some of the larger steps when climbing downhill, as well as during all types of downhill hiking. As a dog intimidator, it was formidable. For that reason alone, it was worth carrying the weight.

My stick came from an uprooted hickory sapling found lying beside the Trail. I wanted a long stick. After I finished cutting and whittling, it measured about six feet. In addition to its use as a support in negotiating rough descents, it worked well in keeping gnats out of my face. I tied my bandanna to my stick at about head high. The sweeping motion in front of my face kept them out of my eyes.

Hiking sticks come in many varieties. Wood is by far the most common. Some people carry store-bought sticks with elaborate carvings and metal tips. Others had bamboo cane poles — seemingly indestructible; however, every time one hit a rock, it sounded like a rifle shot. Some people, including Trail legend Warren Doyle, like ski poles. Ski poles are light, have a point to bury in the earth, and a disk that keeps it from digging in too deeply. It's all a matter of personal preference.

Experiment. Try a hiking stick. If you find it cumbersome, discard it and go without.

9

Injuries & First Aid

"Do not undervalue the headache. While it is at
its sharpest it seems a bad investment; but when
relief begins, the unexpired remainder is worth $4 a minute."
Mark Twain

No piece of hiking equipment is more neglected by thru-hikers than the first aid kit. Perhaps they feel invulnerable to the tragedies that befall mere mortals like weekenders and day-hikers. A more likely reason is that first aid supplies are seldom needed, so thru-hikers tend to forget about replenishment after they are used. Several times I have provided adhesive strips to thru-hikers with blisters. These were experienced hikers who had just "run out" and vowed to get them at the next town, but probably forgot about it. There were also occasions when I dispensed aspirin and antiseptic ointment.

Personally, the first aid problems I encountered were minor, and prompt treatment prevented them from becoming major. This points to reality; when needed, first aid supplies can be extremely important to the hike — if not a life — and must be available.

Hiking the AT is a very strenuous, physically demanding endeavor undertaken during sometimes perilous circumstances. The terrain is rugged. Rocks, roots and dropoffs abound. These factors plus fatigue, extremes of temperature and wet weather provide situations fraught with the possibility of sustaining injury. In situations like these, one must be prepared to deal with injuries as minor as blisters or as serious as broken legs or as life threatening as hypothermia.

Before buying or assembling a first aid kit, it is important to understand the dynamics of the most common injuries suffered by thru-hikers.

BLISTERS

Foot blisters are by far the most common injury suffered by hikers. These result when the foot rubs against the boot, creating friction. This causes the outer layer of skin to move back and forth over the inner layer. Eventually, the two skin layers separate and fluid fills the area where the separation occurs. That is a blister.

The blister problem is exacerbated by wet feet. After a prolonged period of being wet, the skin becomes soft, loses its ability to slide easily inside the sock and becomes much more susceptible to blistering.

The best solution to the blister problem is prevention. Proper fitting boots and two pairs of socks are essential. Keeping feet clean and dry is difficult when hiking all day because of the accumulation of perspiration inside boots. Changing to dry socks helps. However, you can carry only a limited number of socks. During breaks, it helps to remove your boots and let your feet air out.

Blisters signal their development by creating painful hot spots. When this happens, stop hiking and treat the hot spot. Apply tincture of benzoin to the affected area and cover it with mole skin or Second Skin. The mole skin will move inside the sock, thereby eliminating the friction between the skin layers. If the area has already started to blister and the blister is small, treat it in the same way as for a hot spot. Do not open small blisters.

If a large blister develops, the fluid should be removed before the skin breaks. Wash the blister and surrounding area with soap and water. Puncture the bubble at the base with a sterile needle. Gently press the fluid out. Protect the blister and surrounding area by cutting a patch of mole skin or Second Skin larger than the blister area. Cut a donut hole slightly larger than the blister in the mole skin and place the mole skin over the affected area.

If the blister has already broken, treat it like any open wound by washing, applying antiseptic ointment and covering with a sterile bandage.

WOUNDS

How often have you sliced your finger on an open can? More than you care to admit! Right? I have gouged my fingers several times when the can opener on my Swiss Army knife collapsed. I have seen others cut themselves with their knives. On the Trail, cuts and abrasions are everyday occurrences. Proper equipment and materials will keep these wounds clean and protected from infection.

Minor cuts should be gently cleaned and closed. Use Steri-Strips or Coverstrips to close them. Place antiseptic ointment on closed wounds and cover with sterile gauze dressing. Tape the dressing in place.

If the laceration is large and contaminated with dirt or debris, clean the loose dirt and debris from the wound. Do not close the wound. Cover it with a sterile dressing, come off the Trail — and see a doctor.

Abrasions should be thoroughly cleaned, then treated like a cut. Watch for redness, pain or pus — all signs of infection.

SPRAINS

Sprains are injuries to joints, usually ankles and knees, caused by stretching or tearing of ligaments. Most hikers suffer sprains at one time or another. Most are mild to moderate and can be dealt with by wrapping the affected joint with an elastic bandage. Mild and moderate sprains show slight swelling and cause slight pain. In most cases, the victim may continue, gingerly, on his way.

Severe sprains are debilitating and require professional assistance. Victims can expect to leave the Trail and spend considerable time recuperating. These injuries are attended by substantial swelling, purple-blue discoloration and often intense pain.

Severe sprains usually result in immobility. In those cases, the victim will require help in getting back to civilization and care.

STRAINS

Strains are tears in the muscle. Pain is usually localized over the area of the injury. Cold compresses are the best treatment. Keep the painful area inactive. Again, in serious cases, this may mean coming off the Trail. For minor strains, the victim may continue — but do so carefully.

BURNS

Burns on the Trail are usually the result of mishandling a cookpot or getting too close to a wood fire. Usually, the injury is superficial and no treatment is necessary. I often just stick my hand in cold water a few times, and the burn ceases to be a problem. If the burn is of such severity that blistering develops, bubbles should be covered to prevent popping. Douse with cold water, apply aloe and use a nonstick bandage such as Telfa or Second Skin to cover the burn.

Severe burns — skin charred from fire or scalded white and waxy by boiling water — require professional medical attention. The victim should be evacuated immediately for care by a doctor.

SNAKE BITES

I have never met a person who has been bitten by a poisonous snake or a nonpoisonous one for that matter. According to Dr. Vernon G. Vernier, less than 8,000 poisonous snakebites are reported nationwide each year with about five deaths resulting from those bites. There have been no reported cases of snakebites on the AT for more than ten years.

Still, the subject is of great interest to almost everyone along the Trail. I must have been asked at least a hundred times, "Seen any snakes?"

Actually, you will be lucky to see a snake. They will hear you or feel the earth vibrating long before you arrive and will slither out of your way. Occasionally, you may see one — but rarely a poisonous one. I saw only one or two copperheads and no rattlesnakes during my hikes on the AT. I did see a dead timber rattlesnake in Georgia, scared up by a dog and killed by hikers ahead of me, and in Virginia I encountered several rattlesnakes flattened by cars on the Skyline Drive.

There is much controversy about the best method of treating a snakebite. Some experts advise that if you are within an hour's walk of a road, walk out at a moderate pace — and rest often. Don't drink alcohol. Get to a doctor. One source suggests that if walking out is impractical, the next best treatment is to find a cool place and sit it out.

Some people feel the cut and suck treatment can be effective if accomplished directly after being bitten. First, look for fang puncture marks. If none are visible, and after waiting 30 minutes, no inflammation, swelling and severe burning pain develops, it is unlikely that venom has been injected. In that case, simply clean and bandage the wound.

If fang puncture wounds are present and inflammation, swelling and pain occur, venom has been injected. Some contend, that if one acts quickly, it is possible to extract venom from the wound by cutting and sucking. The Cutter Snake Kit contains a cutting blade, three suction cups, a constrictive band and a vial of sterilizing liquid. Instructions accompany the kit, and the user is advised to follow them.

Dr. Fred T. Darvill, Jr. in his book, *Mountaineering Medicine*, indicates that 75 percent of those bitten by pit vipers (all rattlesnakes, copperheads and cotton mouths) will develop "significant problems," and considers snake venom poisoning an emergency. He outlines four procedures to follow in dealing with venomous bites: Retard absorption of the venom, remove the venom from the wound, neutralize the venom, and treat the wound including secondary infection. Dr. Darvill recommends using a Sawyer First Aid Extractor for removal of the venom. He suggests following the instructions that come with the device, except that the device should be left on for ten minutes; then, it should be removed, and the blood and venom disposed of. That done, the device should be reapplied. The process should be repeated for about 40 minutes. After use of the Sawyer device, Dr. Darvill recommends getting the victim to a hospital. Sawyer kits are available through Dynamed or REI of Sumner, Washington.

If symptoms of poisoning appear, Dr. Darvill recommends the

victim lie down and limit use of the bitten area. Jewelry — like rings and bracelets — should be removed before swelling takes place. He also recommends not using the cut and suck treatment, even if the Sawyer device is unavailable. Alcohol or aspirin may hasten the effects of the venom or lead to complications and should not be used. To combat pain, use Tylenol or codeine. If transportation is reasonably available, Dr. Darvill suggests using only a constriction band to retard venom absorption and immediate transportation to the hospital.

Mr. Maynard H. Cox, Director of the North Florida Snakebite Treatment Center and Director of the World Wide Poison Bite Information Center and author of *Protocol for Emergency Room Procedures and Hospital Management of Snakebite* advises otherwise. He contends that snakebite kits are dangerous; they damage tissue, muscles, nerves and veins, and can cause infection. Only two to nine percent of the venom can be extracted by sucking — and then only if done immediately after the bite. According to Cox, the venom from a bite is "walled in" at the site by capillary beds for 12 hours — which means it can't go anywhere.

Mr. Cox contends the most immediate danger to a snakebite victim is from shock and recommends treating the victim for shock, rather than treating for snakebite. He has a beeper and is available at any time for advice on how to respond to a snakebite. He may be reached through the Clay County, Florida, Sheriff's Department at (904) 264-6512. According to Mr. Cox, proper treatment for snakebite consists of the administration of anti-venom, antibiotics and a tetanus shot.

During my hikes of the AT, I did not carry a snakebite kit nor did anyone else I knew. I would, however, carry Mr. Cox's beeper number with me in my first aid packet. As in any physical injury situation, the key is in prevention. In this case, look carefully before you put you arms, legs or bottom anywhere.

ANIMAL BITES

About the only animal bites the thru-hiker should worry about are from dogs. Obviously, there is always the chance encounter with a rabid fox, raccoon, skunk or bat. But that is remote. No one I met on the Trail had suffered bites from any of these animals. However, a couple of hikers were bitten by dogs.

In the event of a bite, treat it like any other puncture wound. Clean and sterilize it, apply antibiotic salve and bandage it. If you suspect that the animal is rabid, capture it, if you can (safely), and take it and yourself promptly to the hospital. Otherwise, just get *yourself* to the hospital.

INSECT BITES/STINGS

You will be besieged by insects on the AT. They are a fact of life, and most are harmless. Gnats were the most bothersome for me, constantly flying around my head and diving into my eyes. My eye would sting for a few minutes until tears washed the carcass out. But gnats were not a health problem.

Mosquitoes were a problem only in certain areas. The tent provided adequate protection from them. No-see-ums, not a problem during the daytime, occasionally appeared at night. Tents are also effective against them. Otherwise, get into your sleeping bag.

Wild honey bees are another story. Encounters with them were sporadic. Mostly they fly around, then buzz off. On one occasion, however, they did swarm at a shelter where I was staying. They literally covered me, my equipment, pack, sleeping bag and clothes. It was a bit tricky getting dressed and out of there without a bee under my collar or under a pack strap. Yellow jackets can be a real problem. Several of my Trail acquaintances were stung, as were some young hikers from a summer camp. They had the misfortune of sitting on a log housing a yellow jacket nest. When I encountered them further down the Trail, they were swinging like wind — gusted windmills at anything with wings. Yellow jackets congregate around shelters where they feed on leftovers, cans and debris left by campers and hikers. Sometimes eating without swallowing a yellow jacket becomes an accomplishment!

If stung, remove the stinger promptly and gently by scraping it out with a fingernail. Pinching it out may only imbed it further. After removal, apply aspirin topically to the area. To accomplish this: grind the aspirin into a powder, place it on the sting, add a little water and smear it. Aloe also helps, I am told, as does juice from the jewel weed, wild impatiens.

Fragrant lotions and soaps attract bees and yellow jackets as do perfumes, fruit and syrups. Sunrise and sunset are the insects' high stress periods when they are most likely to become aggressive. Be most careful during these times.

I had several instances of ticks on my body. While none were serious, several did manage to get their heads under my skin. The easiest method of removal is to grab the tick's body with a pair of tweezers, and pull up and over. That should disgorge the tick. Then, apply a little antibiotic and an adhesive strip. (Don't use the lit cigarette to the tick's butt trick. It may imbed the tick's head more deeply.) If you are passing through tick country, check yourself frequently. Ticks are easiest to remove before they burrow.

HYPOTHERMIA

Hypothermia, the most serious threat to life and health on the Trail, has claimed a number of lives on the AT. Its danger is it can occur under conditions not normally considered threatening. Deaths have occurred at temperatures as high as 42 degrees and at sea level. Hypothermia can creep up unexpectedly, particularly when one is exhausted, sick, lacking nourishment or all of the above.

Hypothermia is the result of body heat being lost more quickly than the body can replace it. Wet clothing increases heat loss. Wind chill aggravates the problem. The condition first affects the extremities. Then, core body temperature begins to drop, vital organs become affected and death ensues.

The onset of hypothermia can be recognized when victims begin acting stupidly, don't eat, become uncoordinated, speak unusually slowly and shiver uncontrollably. Such symptoms occur even in mild cases, warning that immediate steps need to be taken to prevent a worse situation from developing.

Basic treatment for hypothermia is prevention. Do not get overly fatigued. Wear appropriate clothing, polypro and wool, and outer, waterproof, wind-resistant garments. Eat frequently to maintain an acceptable metabolic rate. Camp early. Maintain body heat by starting a fire; huddle together if hiking with a partner. Do whatever is necessary to reduce heat loss.

If hypothermia symptoms appear, get into warm dry clothing or inside a sleeping bag. Drink warm, sweetened fluids. Get the core body warmed first, and as rapidly as possible.

One technique may be for two people to get into the sleeping bag with the victim — and maintain skin-to-skin body contact. If the condition is not too severe, encourage the victim to exercise. This may help to reheat the internal organs — or at least, keep the core temperature from falling below the critical point.

HEAT EXHAUSTION

Heat exhaustion accompanies strenuous activity in a hot environment. It is usually associated with failure to replace liquid lost through perspiration. Common symptoms are malaise, palpitations, faintness, nausea, weakness, headache and muscle cramps.

The condition is usually not serious, but it can progress to heat stroke if not treated. Treatment is best obtained by lying down in a cool place and drinking one-to-two quarts of cool water with a small amount of salt (one-half teaspoon). Loosen or remove clothing. Sprinkle water to enhance evaporation and cool the body. Placing cold water compresses on exposed skin serves the same purpose.

HEAT STROKE

This stage follows heat exhaustion. It is dangerous because the body is producing more heat than can be dissipated. Symptoms are: a sense of warmth; hot, red, dry skin; confusion; headache; extremely rapid pulse; staggering and eventual coma. Sweating is absent or reduced. Body temperature reaches 105 to 106 degrees.

This is a medical emergency. Body temperature must be lowered immediately. Immerse victim in a cold body of water, stream, lake or pond. Apply cold water until body temperature returns to normal. Place victim in cool shady location. Get victim to professional medical care as soon as movement is possible.

LIGHTNING

Lightning can be a formidable terror, particularly to one caught in a thunderstorm on a 5,000 foot ridge. I have seen a small tree actually explode from a lightning strike.

If you see or hear a storm approaching, leave the ridge or summit. Judge your distance from a storm by watching for the flash of lightning and counting the seconds until you hear the thunder. Divide that by five, and that will give you the distance in miles from the lightning. Thunderstorms often move with amazing speed, so take immediate action and seek protection. That can be difficult. An open area with some shrubs away from large trees is desirable. Gently sloping ground is better than steep slopes. Stay away from rock overhangs or shallow caves. Get low to the ground, squat on your Ensolite pad well away from your pack with its metal frame and utensils. The pad acts as insulation to protect against grounding.

FIRST AID KITS

Backpacker first aid kits can be purchased off the shelf or can be personally assembled. Included in off the shelf models are physician-designed creations like Indiana Camp Supply and Adventure Medical Kits. Indiana Camp Supply's premier model weighs six pounds, costs $410, and contains almost enough equipment and supplies to outfit a field hospital. They also offer a more basic kit, the Ultima model, weighing three pounds and costing $188. Adventure Medical Kits (AMK) of Berkeley, California, sells several models, including the Comprehensive, the Backcountry, the Fundamentals and the Daytripper. Weights range from almost three pounds to six ounces and prices range from $130 to $26. Recreational Equipment, Incorporated (REI) also offers several kits: First Essential, First Essential Lite and the Basic. These kits range in price from $48 down to $10 and weigh from one pound, six ounces to ten ounces.

Atway Carey, Ltd. makes kits called the Trekker, the Expedition and the Backpacker. Prices range from $15 to $96. Weights are from two pounds six ounces to four pounds five ounces.

Whatever your choice, be sure you know the contents and how to use them. Read the directions.

For those desiring to make their own kit, a few essential items include:

- wound closure strips
- Tylenol (acetaminophen, if you buy generic drugs)
- adhesive strips;
- Imodium (loperamide HCL)
- non-adherent adhesive pads (Telfa)
- gauze roll
- gauze pads
- irrigation syringe
- absorbent pads
- tincture of benzoin
- elastic bandages
- tape
- safety pins
- triangular bandages
- scissors
- tweezers
- antiseptic ointment
- aspirin
- mole skin/Second Skin

Most pros suggest buying a kit from one of the suppliers like AMK, REI or Indiana Camp Supply. These will be more complete than do-it-yourself kits, they come with directions and will be less expensive because such companies buy in bulk and pass along the savings. Top of the line kits will also contain more specialized supplies and equipment than one is likely to include in a self-produced kit.

Food & Water

"Edible. Good to eat and wholesome to digest as a
worm to a toad, a toad to a snake, a snake to a
pig, a pig to a man, a man to a worm."
Ambrose Bierce

FOOD

"What do you eat?" This is a question most familiar to thru-hikers. The answer? Every diet is tailor-made and varies widely from person-to-person. On the Trail, it is no different. Thru-hikers eat a variety of concoctions that depend mostly on food availability. For those having recently received parcels in the mail, diets reflect the ambitious initial meal planning and often "delicacies" not normally available at small general stores. Those who do not have recent mail drops are forced to rely on the sometimes sparse and limited inventories of small stores. In your initial planning, forget about "living off the land," or of supplementing your diet with foods gathered in the wild. To do that requires specific knowledge about plants and animals indigenous to a region, and very few have such detailed knowledge. Second, the time and effort needed to hunt or gather food sufficient to meet caloric requirements is prohibitive. Third, there is already too much population pressure on the Trail. To add foraging by thousands of hikers would be an unconscionable burden on the land from an ethical viewpoint.

When planning daily menus, a thru-hiker must consider: (1) the body's caloric requirements; (2) the body's individual ability to use various foods; and (3) the ability to carry those foods for sustained periods of time.

The main factor influencing diet planning is availability. Remember, resupply is difficult. The Trail is located on the heights of land far from population centers. Rarely, even in small towns, will the thru-hiker have access to a supermarket and must depend on what can be purchased from "mom and pop general stores" with limited food inventories.

A second possibility for resupply is the mail drop. Parcels of food or other items may be sent ahead to various post offices along the Trail. Such parcels should be addressed to yourself c/o General Delivery with the name of the town and the zip code. Across the top write: **Please Hold for Appalachian Trail Hiker** and expected date of arrival. Postal rules require the postmaster to hold such parcels for 30 days — not a long period for a thru-hiker. However, most postmasters voluntarily extend that period to accommodate hikers. The postmaster in Damascus, Virginia, held a parcel for me for over 45 days, and in Atkins, Virginia, it was over 60 days. Of course, I wrote and kept them informed of my progress.

Appendix II contains a list of post offices, their distances from the Trail and telephone numbers for in-person coordination concerning hours of operation and policies.

You should realize that coming off the Trail for a food drop or for a food purchase can be an exercise in itself. Many facilities are two, three or more miles from the Trail which means hiking four or more miles to resupply. Some hikers hitchhike. But I don't recommended it. A technique sometimes used by hikers to save time and energy is to hide their packs near the road and walk unencumbered into town.

The food required for a day on the Trail generally weighs about two pounds. Consequently, with all the other supplies and equipment, a hiker can expect to comfortably carry about a ten-day supply of food. That means resupply is necessary every eight-to-ten days. The drawback to mail drops is that post offices reasonably close to the Trail are seldom located eight or ten days apart. Another problem is the difficulty of planning where you will be after the first couple of weeks. That means, in realistic terms, that someone else must periodically mail your parcels. Predetermined schedules can be difficult to coordinate and maintain.

The first question a novice hiker asks is, "How much and what kind of food should I carry?" The answer is, "It depends." It depends on body size, physical condition at the start and how much weight you're willing to carry. The bottom line is realizing that thru-hiking requires a tremendous amount of energy, calculated in the form of calories. For example, the U.S. Army lists dietary requirements for soldiers participating in "strenuous duty" up to 4,500 calories per day. Thru-hikers can expect to require a similar amount. Obviously, the more weight, the longer the day, the tougher the terrain and the colder the weather, the higher the caloric requirements.

Calories derive from three categories of foods: carbohydrates, protein and fats. According to the National Academy of Sciences, carbohydrates comprise about 46 percent of the average American's diet. They are the quickest source of energy, since they are digested more rapidly than protein or fat. The principle sources of carbohydrates are sugars (glucose and fructose) and starches.

Proteins are a complex biological substance composed of amino acids, the building blocks of the various cells that comprise our bodies. Proteins come from animal and vegetable sources. Meat, fish, milk products and eggs are the main animal sources. Whole grains, legumes (peas and beans) and nuts constitute the most common vegetable sources. The body uses only limited amounts of protein, about 45 grams per day for a 155 pound man. Any amount above what is needed by the body is converted to glycogen which is then stored as fat. Protein is used by the body throughout the day, so protein should be eaten at regular intervals rather than at one concentrated sitting.

Fats are a concentrated source of energy. A single gram of fat produces more than twice the calories of carbohydrates or protein of the same weight. Fats, because they take longer to digest than carbohydrates or proteins, have a longer satiation value. Some backpackers suggest that as much as 35-to-40 percent of a thru-hiker's diet should be fat. Others suggest that consumption of fats should approach zero. Nutritionists reflect a similarly wide divergence of views. There is a middle ground, however. A sizeable number of hikers and nutritionists think the hiker should decide how much or how little fat to consume. Caveats to this advice admonish people not to eat more than the body's caloric requirement and that they remain physically active (really not a concern to a thru-hiker).

From a practical standpoint, anyone planning a menu for thru-hiking can discard all the exotic recipes for banana nut bread, reflected oven baking, and other time and resource-consuming dishes found in some trail food manuals. Focus should concentrate on creating one-pot meals. Noodles, spaghetti, rice, instant potatoes, peas, beans, lentils, macaroni, cheese, canned tuna, chicken, turkey and ham plus smoked sausage or salami. Flavor enhancers can be used in various combinations to make meals more appetizing and satisfying. The only limit is your imagination and courage to experiment. One last piece of advice: get out the campstove and cook pot. Start experimenting with different foods before you get on the Trail. You will quickly learn what suits your tastes.

Commercially prepared, dehydrated meats are expensive and often not available. I used a cheaper, though heavier alternative: six ounce cans of meat. The major disadvantage was this required packing out the empty cans. To save space, I crushed the cans between rocks and placed them in a Ziploc bag until I could discard them. The Ziploc bag kept food or juice from soiling the pack. All ingredients mentioned above can be obtained at most stores in the Trail's vicinity.

My all-time favorite called for Lipton Butter and Herb noodles supplemented with an extra cup of macaroni along with a bullion cube, a clove of garlic and a six ounce can of meat, usually chicken, turkey or ham. First, I filled my cook pot half full of water (about three cups), added the meat, garlic, bullion cube and brought it to a boil. Next I added the pasta and allowed it to cook for eight-to-ten minutes, or until the noodles were soft. Sometimes I added a small onion in place of the garlic.

Another dish contained smoked sausage or salami, onions or garlic and a dried soup mix consisting of dried beans, peas, carrots and pasta. This recipe was prepared in the same manner as the noodle dish but took longer to cook. Other single-pot possibilities include:

macaroni, tuna or meat, cheese and instant milk or instant potatoes, meat, instant milk, gravy mix and onion.

After some time on the Trail, even the best of dishes can become boring. To improve flavor and add variety, carry different seasonings. Add a little pesto or oregano and basil to pasta for an Italian flair. Add curry to chicken and rice or perhaps a gravy mix. Make powdered onion and powdered garlic a staple in your food sack. These spice up a one-pot meal, are light and take up little room in a pack.

Not all meals are suppers. In the morning, you want to eat, break camp, and be on your way with a minimum of fuss. Instant oatmeal, instant coffee, tea or chocolate, and instant milk over gorp (a trail mix containing dried fruit, granola, peanuts and candy-covered chocolate pieces) are time savers. Also, All Bran cereal can help balky bowels, especially at the beginning of your hike when your body is trying to adjust to its new schedule. For lunches, I ate canned tuna fish or sardines with peanut butter crackers and gorp. I ate cold food rather than take time from hiking to prepare a hot meal. Most thru-hikers do the same. However, some prefer a hot meal; Lipton, Knorr or Campbell soup mixes alone or with meat added make a great hot lunch.

Some hikers advocate do-it-yourself food dehydration ahead-of-time. But for a thru-hiker, the practicality is directly related to the use of mail drops. If you plan in detail and rely extensively on mail drops, it is an ideal solution to resupply. If you don't plan using mail drops extensively, forget it.

Normally, I carried enough food for five or six days with one day extra for emergency purposes. I planned my resupply using a combination of mail drops (very few) and purchases from stores close to the Trail. I used the *Appalachian Trail Data Book* extensively in planning my resupply. It contains a detailed list of terrain features crossed by the Trail. Where the Trail crosses roads, codes indicate the direction and distances to: groceries, supplies, lodging, restaurants and post offices. It is very important to carry one of these guides. (Available through the Appalachian Trail Conference for $3.95 or $3.35 for members.)

A single pot served for food preparation. I ate directly from the pot, thereby eliminating the need for plates. One plastic cup served for drinks, and a spoon and a fork for eating. My pocket-knife served very well for food preparation. That was my entire kitchen, except for a plastic scrub pad for cleaning up.

I found that separating my food into plastic bags labeled for breakfast, lunch or supper served to organize my pantry and reduced the need to rummage through one big food sack in search of ingredients for a meal.

WATER

Finding water in the mountains, unless during a prolonged dry spell, is usually not a problem. The major source of concern about water along the Trail is purity. A number of microorganisms can cause sickness. Some of these are:

- *Bacteria* — range from 0.2 to 10 micron in size and can cause a number of illnesses ranging from food poisoning to typhoid fever.
- *Protozoa* — single-cell, hard-shell parasites that range from 2 to 15 microns in size. Two that affect U.S. water are *giardia lamblia*, one of the most common waterborne parasites, and *cryptosporidium*, which can be spread for two months after symptoms disappear in the host. Some infected people never show symptoms of the sickness. It cannot be destroyed by iodine. Only boiling or filters with an absolute pore size of 1 micron or smaller are effective.
- *Viruses* — the smallest of waterborne illness causers, 0.004 to 0.1 micron. Viruses cause diseases such as polio and hepatitis. There is disagreement in the scientific community on the prevalence of these dangerous microorganisms in U.S. waters, but they are certainly a larger danger in some foreign areas. Best protection against these viruses is innoculation.

Not classified as microorganisms, but certainly dangerous to health, nonetheless, are pollutants from organic chemicals: herbicides, pesticides, fertilizer, fuel or strip-mine runoff. All byproducts of agricultural and industrial activity pose problems in nearby waters. Needless to say, hikers should not use water from such areas.

Most shelters along the Trail are sited near springs where water runs directly from the ground. In such cases it is usually okay to drink such water untreated, which I did for 2,000 miles; and I suffered no ill effects. However, in our "always err on the side of safety" society, the rule is to treat or boil all untreated water. If the water comes from a surface source (stream, pond, lake), it must certainly be treated. I *always* boiled such water.

The protozoan *giardia lamblia*, or *giardia*, as it is known, is the most prevalent parasite in waters of the Appalachians. They come from the feces of native animals, farm animals and humans. Drinking as little as six *giardia* cysts can cause infection. It takes from six to 20 days after infection for symptoms to begin. Diarrhea, abdominal cramps, fatigue and vomiting may start. Symptoms normally last from ten to 14 days and can be treated with prescription drugs. Fortunately, only about 25 percent of those infected develop symptoms (fortunate, unless you fall within the 25 percent).

There are several methods and devices that can help defend against parasites in water. These are:

- Bottle filters. The filter is built into the cap. Simply scoop up water, put on cap, and drink.
- Chemical treatment. Use chlorine dioxide to disinfect water. Useful against *giardia* and *cryptosporidium*.
- Gravity-feed filters. Fill filter reservoir and hang from a tree. Water trickles into the container.
- Iodine. Add liquid, tablet or crystal to water. Wait for 20 minutes before drinking. Iodine does not kill *cryptosporidium*. It tastes terrible. Some products come with a "neutralizer" that mask the odor and unpleasant taste.
- Pump filter. Drop intake hose into a water source, the other end into a container and start pumping. These filters are faster and more efficient than gravity feeders, but they plug up and require maintenance. The filter material consists mostly of ceramics, fiber glass, glass fiber, depth filter or carbon. Carbon, in conjunction with other materials, removes herbicides, pesticides and chlorine. Ceramics snare microorganisms as water passes through. They are long lasting and can be cleaned repeatedly

before replacement is necessary. But they are brittle and fragile and need careful handling, particularly in cold weather. Most modern filters are depth filters that strain microorganisms through thick elements as water is pumped through. These can be cleaned with a brush or back flushed. Fiber glass or glass fibers are long and slick and can be molded into structures that catch impurities.

It is important to know how long the filters will function before needing replacement. Some filters are now equipped with pre-filters, small devices that attach to the filter's intake hose and strains out larger particles that would plug up the main filter. These devices prolong filter life, which is quite important, because some filters are very expensive. Jury-rigged prefilters are also effective. Wrap a coffee filter or a handkerchief over the intake nozzle and secure with rubber bands or other device to hold material in place.

Backpacker water filters weigh, on average, between a pound and a pound and a half, and cost from around $50 for one with a four-micron filter (good for *giardia* whose width is five microns) to $200 for a 0.2 micron filter (good for even the smallest bacteria and some larger viruses). Manufacturers include: First Need, Katahdyn, MSR, PUR, Exstream Water Technologies and General Ecology. The Katadyn Pocket Filter comes highly recommended but with a steep price tag of $199. McNett Aquamira Water Treatment kit uses chlorine dioxide that comes in a two-shirt-pocket-sized bottle system. WPC's Potable Agua remains the mainstay of the iodine treatment systems.

After climbing mountains all day, the last thing a thru-hiker wants is to be climbing half a mile down a mountain to a water source and back several times during the evening and again in the morning.

To eliminate those trips, I bought a collapsible two and a half-gallon water bag that I filled and hung from a tree or a nail on the shelter wall. A bag with a nylon outer shell holds up best to rough usage. A spigot at the bottom of the bag allows easy control of the water spout. This provided enough water for supper, for cleaning utensils, breakfast the next morning and filling canteens. When ready to break camp, simply empty the excess water, fold the bag and put it in your pack. For fear of contamination, I did not use the bag for water from surface sources.

11

Animals on the Trail

"The scapegoat of olden times, driven for the
bystanders sins, has become a tender thing, a running
injury. There, running away . . . is me:
hurt it and you are hurting me."
Edward Hoagland

The thru-hiker can expect to see a wide range of wildlife in the mountains. Many mammals, reptiles and birds seldom seen in urbanized communities can often be observed by alert hikers. Hikers experience different emotions in their contact with animals. Some, particularly those who enjoy hunting, may find it invigorating in a primordial sense to watch a mature deer or a bear, unaware of human presence, going about the business of survival in the wild. Conversely, the trusting innocence welling from the liquid eyes of an orphaned fawn will invoke feelings of tenderness from even those with the fiercest predatory instincts. Some will experience exhilaration watching a great raptor, an eagle or perhaps a hawk, floating easily along the updrafts — until a glimpse of prey sends it suddenly diving earthward. Others will shudder with concern for the hapless target, a rabbit or mouse perhaps, foraging for food, unaware of impending doom. And there will be so many opportunities to see squirrels and rabbits; this will become ordinary. For others, an overnight in a shelter will afford more than enough contact with mice.

The great advantage man has as predator-in-chief is being universally feared by all animals in the wild. A hiker in the Appalachians need not fear any of the animals with whom he or she comes in contact. No animal found along the AT will attack a human being unless cornered or in some way provoked. The exception to this rule is an encounter with a rabid animal. Rabies causes animals to act in bizarre ways.

Animals are extremely fearful of people and will leave an area at the first indication of human presence. Because most animals have superior senses of hearing and smell, they will almost always detect a human before the human sees them. This makes it difficult to see the most wary animals.

Certain weather conditions help equalize the odds. During periods of mist or during and just after rain, the forest is damp. This dampness muffles sound. Also, when the forest is damp the wind is usually still. Muffled sound does not carry and still wind does not broadcast scent, so a hiker is often able to approach wild animals undetected. I have seen many deer, wild turkeys and bears, during these periods.

Although man sits at the top of the predator chain, that does not automatically endow him with "divine right of kings" in dealing with the lesser creatures who share our planet. Our position imposes on us the unique requirement to exercise our humanity. The guiding rule in dealing with animals in the wild is to exercise reason. Enjoy observing animals, respect the natural environment that is their habitat and — above all, *leave them alone*.

Animals are fallible creatures. They do dumb things or act out of character, just like people. I vividly remember a fat gray squirrel jumping from limb-to-limb through the tree canopy above me while I was walking the Trail in Virginia. It mistimed or misjudged a jump, slipped off a branch and landed with a loud thud on the Trail about five feet in front of me. The squirrel, apparently none the worse from its fall, instantly gathered itself together, and scampered up the nearest tree and out of sight before I could recover from my amazement.

On another occasion I was "attacked" by a grouse. Now everyone knows that grouse don't attack people. They fly from danger. So you can imagine my perplexity when this grouse, neck feathers flared, came charging towards me hissing like a snake. It came within four or five feet, backed off slightly, then feigned another attack. A second later, a little ball of feathers tumbled from the grass beside the path and passed directly between my legs. A baby grouse! Here was a mother at great risk to herself simply trying to divert my attention from her baby. After the baby had reentered the thick grass behind me, the mother grouse gave me the "broken wing" routine in an attempt to lure me away.

Below are listed the animals that one is most likely to encounter during a thru-hike. Included is some basic information to help in identifying them with certain characteristics or traits which should be of more than just casual interest.

SNAKES

The one animal that provokes the most interest, and in many cases, totally unreasonable fear and repulsion among hikers and the people along the Trail, is the snake. The woods are really not teeming with evil snakes waiting to sink their fangs into unsuspecting people.

I saw many snakes on the Trail. They were, with two exceptions, all nonpoisonous. The reality is: Hikers will see very few poisonous species of snakes. The only venomous snakes known to inhabit the Appalachian Mountains are —
Copperheads
Timber rattlesnakes
Eastern diamondback rattlesnakes
Pigmy rattlesnakes
Massasauga rattlesnakes and
Cottonmouths.
Copperheads and timber rattlesnakes are found all along the Trail from Georgia to Maine but rarely north of Massachusetts. Eastern diamondback rattlesnakes are found along the Trail only in Georgia and North Carolina; pigmy rattlesnakes from Tennessee south; cottonmouths from Virginia south; and the Massasauga rattlesnake in New York and Pennsylvania. Cottonmouths like warm water and are found infrequently in the mountains. Eastern diamondback rattlesnakes, the largest of

the snakes (up to eight feet), are quite rare.

These snakes all belong to the group known as pit vipers. They have lorel pits (heat sensors) in their heads that sense and locate warmblooded animals up to 14 feet away in total darkness. All snakes are sensitive to vibrations in the earth. Pit vipers are most readily recognized by their triangular-shaped heads. Rattlesnakes are identified by the rattles at the ends of their tails. The copperhead has brown or copper-colored hourglass-shaped patterns on its back, perfect camouflage among dried leaves.

Pit vipers normally hunt along trails or game paths for small rodents. That will be the only time you will see them, unless you find them sunning themselves on a rock.

All snakes, and pit vipers especially, are timid where people are concerned. When people approach they usually lie low or move out of the danger zone. Only when surprised or cornered are they likely to be dangerous; but as a rule, they will not attack unless provoked. Rattlesnakes tend to give warning by rattling their tails.

When walking in likely snake territory be alert. It is wise to advertise your approach. Kick or push aside with your hiking stick any brush or leaves that cover the path. When snakes know you are coming they will most likely slither out of your way.

Snakes often sun themselves on rocky promontories or ledges. Be careful when climbing around these areas. Should you encounter a poisonous snake by surprise, you can easily outdistance it in about three steps. Don't freeze. Move immediately and quickly away.

The AT passes through the habitat of a large number of nonpoisonous snakes. Those that a hiker is most apt to meet are —
Garter snakes
Black snakes
Corn snakes and
Water snakes.

You will see many of these snakes, particularly garter snakes and black snakes. The corn snake has markings similar to the copperhead and is often mis-identified. Nonpoisonous snakes prey on small rodents, frogs and lizards. They occupy an important place in the ecosystem as do the pit vipers. Don't bother them, and they won't bother you. (See Chapter 9 for what to do in case of a venomous snakebite.)

BEARS

Bears hold a special place in people's hearts. After all, we grew up with a Teddy bear in our cribs or playpens and were read the story of "Goldilocks and the Three Bears." Later, we met Smoky Bear, Yogi Bear and other anthropomorphic bears.

A visit to the bear cage at a zoo did much to put live bears in a realistic perspective for me. The reality is: Bears are not lovable, cuddly, fuzzy, little replicas of ourselves. They are powerful, wild animals ruled by instinct and the primal urge to survive. In the backcountry, when a human being is perceived by a hungry bear as a competitor for food, the human is in danger — and the human should understand this.

Black bears are not as large as grizzlies; still their size is formidable. Four to five hundred pounds is not unusual. While they have very keen hearing and a superb sense of smell, their eyesight is strangely limited. I have been as close as 30 yards to a bear in open forest. The bear, looking dead in my direction, was unable to see me.

Fortunately, black bears — the only kind found in the east — are much smaller and less aggressive than the grizzly bear. Black bear attacks on humans are very rare. But as people have encroached deeper into bear habitat, and bears have come into increasingly close contact with humans, particularly human food, unfortunate incidents between bears and people have begun to increase. There have recently been a couple of incidents in national parks where bears have mauled hikers and one death has been reported. Bears are hunted outside of the national parks and give humans a wide berth. However, in the Great Smoky Mountains and the Shenandoah National Parks, hunting is not allowed, and that has caused some bears to lose their fear of man. Bears have learned that people with packs can be a source of food.

This does not mean that bears will attack you if you are carrying a pack. In my several bear encounters in the Smokies and the Shenandoah National Park, the bears mostly avoided me. They either slipped off the Trail or ran away in obvious fright. Other hikers have had similar experiences. But there are reports of bears scaring hikers into dropping their packs.

As much as 90 percent of a black bear's diet is vegetation: berries, sedges (rush-like plants) and grasses. But they are omnivorous and will eat meat when it is available — or people food like noodles, rice or spaghetti. Bears are good swimmers and adept at catching fish. Rotten logs containing grubs, beetles, crickets and worms are favorite feeding sites. They will also rip apart honey beehives and endure the stings for the honey, bees and larvae.

When it comes to food in the national parks bears are opportunists if not outright connivers. They are quick to tear up an unattended pack or take food from a campsite. That is the point at which bears and humans become competitors for food. In this case, it is better to let the bear win.

To reduce the possibilities for conflict between bears and people, the National Park Service (NPS) has constructed chain-link fencing barriers across the fronts of the shelters in the Smokies. This keeps the bears out, providing the doors are closed. Hikers are warned not to leave packs unattended and to keep the shelter doors closed. In Shenandoah National Park, the NPS has erected steel poles with prongs at the top. Gaffs are provided to lift packs or food sacks onto the prongs. The poles keep packs or food high enough off the ground where they cannot be reached by bears.

If confronted by an aggressive bear, practice the following DON'TS. Don't panic. Don't run. You cannot outrun a bear unless you can do better than 30 miles an hour. Don't climb a tree. Black bears are very adept at climbing trees. Don't look the bear in the eye. That is considered aggressive behavior by bears, and you definitely do not want to appear aggressive at this time.

The best solution in the face of an aggressive bear is to lie on the ground in a fetal position; protect your face and neck with your arms. If you do that, most likely the bear will not bother you.

If you are outside a national park and there are no bear restraints or poles, the best way to protect your food from bears and other critters — raccoons, porcupines, skunks or any other marauders — is to hang your food sack from a tree.

Many camping and hiking books indicate that you should select two trees fairly close together, run a rope between them and hang your food from the rope. This is great on theory but short in practice. I can't remember ever camping in a place with two trees reasonably spaced that were climbable.

A better solution is to find a tree with a stout, four-to-five inch diameter branch about 20 feet from the ground. About ten feet out from the trunk, throw a rope over the branch and haul your food sack ten or 12 feet above the ground. You can either tie the rope off on the tree trunk or — better yet — tie a sack of equal weight to the other end of the rope and adjust the rope so that both sacks are at least ten feet off the ground. You will need some type of gaff, stout stick or a line to retrieve the sacks in the morning.

COYOTES

Long considered a western animal, the coyote has extended its range and is now found along the entire Appalachian chain. In some areas, the coyote has interbred with dogs producing offspring known as coydogs, which are as wild as coyotes.

Pure coyotes stand about two feet tall at the shoulder. Their coat is normally a grizzled gray or a reddish gray, and their tails are bushy and black tipped. They are about four feet long and weigh between 20 and 40 pounds. Coydogs are usually larger and normally lack the dark vertical line on the lower foreleg.

Because the coyote is very wary, it is seldom seen. Its main prey is small rodents, birds, eggs and young or injured deer. Actually, they will eat carrion or anything with fur, feathers or scales. They have been known to attack mature deer. They are terrified of man and present no danger to a hiker.

A coyote will sometimes follow a trail behind a hiker hoping to pick up a morsel of food. But the interval between hiker and coyote will be at least 30 minutes; in fact, it is unlikely the hiker will ever see the coyote.

Once I was fortunate. I saw one on the ridge south of Stecoah Gap, North Carolina. Its attention was focused on a dog coming up the Trail from the opposite direction. Since it was upwind of me, it was unaware of my approach. I rapped my stick on a rock before I came too close, and the sound sent it racing headlong in flight down the mountain.

FOXES

The mountains are full of fox, but they, like the coyote, are secretive; you will rarely see one. A fox's diet consists of small rodents, rabbits, woodchucks, mice and squirrels as well as birds, eggs and carrion. They also feed heavily on vegetation such as berries, grapes and apples during the summer. About a quarter of their diet consists of crickets, caterpillars, grasshoppers and crayfish. They also will occasionally follow a hiker hoping to find dropped or abandoned food.

The two species of fox most likely to be encountered are the red fox and the gray fox. The red fox is easily recognized by its reddish fur and the white tip on its bushy tail. The gray fox has a grayish cast to its fur and a black tip at the tail. Foxes are little more than foot high at the shoulder and weigh between eight and 15 pounds, much smaller than a coyote. Foxes are vulnerable to rabies, and those who exhibit strange behavior should be avoided.

WOLVES

For 750,000 years the red wolf was the dominant predator in the eastern U.S. However, man waged a relentless war on the red wolf, driving it to the brink of extinction. It has been 100 years since the wolf last traveled through the mountains.

The NPS and the U.S. Fish and Wildlife Service in 1991 attempted to reintroduce the wolf back into the Great Smoky Mountains. Unfortunately, after eight years the program was terminated. Low pup survival and the inability of the wolves to establish a home range in the park were cited as the main reasons for the failure of the program.

BOBCATS

A fifty pound bobcat is a formidable predator. Actually, it ranges in size from 15 to 70 pounds. Tawny in color with mottled brown spots, a signature bobbed or stubby tail and distinctly tufted ears, it is found throughout the mountains.

Bobcats hunt almost exclusively at night for their main prey, hare and rabbit, but they also eat mice, porcupines, squirrels and cave bats. Unless prey is unavailable, they seldom eat carrion. Occasionally, a bobcat will prey upon livestock, particularly poultry.

I have observed a bobcat watching a group of grouse from its perch on a tree stump, hoping the grouse would come within range. My appearance surprised the cat, and it leaped silently off the stump to slip out of sight. I was fortunate. Bobcats are seldom seen.

WILD BOARS

Wild boars are related to the domestic pig. There the similarity ends. Boars have stocky bodies with dark grizzled hair and long heads with tough cartilaginous snouts, short legs and straight tails. Their hooves are cloven. Upper tusks, modified canine teeth, curl up and out along the side of the mouth; these can be up to nine inches long. Lower canines are smaller, turn out slightly outside the mouth and curl back toward the eye; these are used to root though the forest floor in search of food but are also very effective weapons; large predators usually pass them up in favor of easier prey. A few full-grown males can weigh up to 400 pounds. However, most boars top out at about 350 pounds.

Boars were initially introduced into the United States from European stock imported for hunting purposes. Initially confined to hunting preserves, many escaped and interbred with feral descendents of domestic pigs. Pure-blooded boars, however, do still exist, mainly in eastern Tennessee and western North Carolina, primarily in the Nantahala and Cherokee National Forests. In the Great Smoky Mountain National Park their numbers have increased to the point that they present an ecological problem; boars compete with deer and bear for food, and their rooting tears sod, making the balds susceptible to seeding and subsequent forestation. The boars' main diet consists of acorns, pecan, hickory and beech nuts. When nuts are scarce they will eat a wide range of vegetation, including grass, roots, tubers and berries. They have also been known to eat crayfish, snakes, salamanders, frogs, and the eggs and young of ground-nesting birds as well as young rabbits and carrion. Reports also indicate boars have killed and eaten fawns.

Hikers are most likely to see boars in the Great Smoky

Mountains National Park. The many torn-up patches of forest floor present visual evidence of their foraging expeditions. I observed a family group of six piglets accompanied by two sows near Derrick Knob Shelter in the Smokies. The boars, spread out almost in a skirmish line, rooted their snouts through the leaves, as they made their way up the hill. After they had passed, the forest floor resembled a test site for Roto-tillers.

RACCOONS

Raccoons are native only to the Americas. Ranging from two-to-three feet long, eight-to-16 inches tall and weighing up to 48 pounds, the raccoon is mostly nocturnal. Often raccoons can be seen at dusk as they begin their foraging. They will eat just about anything. In the wild, their diet includes grubs, grasshoppers, crickets, nuts and grapes, small rodents such as deer mice and voles, bird's eggs and young birds as well as frogs, crayfish, turtles, clams, worms and fish. They are most often observed near wooded streams.

Raccoons avoid people. However, in places where they are protected, they become quite brazen and will become pests. To protect food from raccoons, use the same procedure as for bears. Get the food sack off the ground but also away from tree branches where raccoons can get to it. Raccoons generally avoid shelters along the Trail.

Don't forget, though, raccoons are tough fighters and can easily defeat a single dog. If cornered, they can be very dangerous.

PORCUPINES

Porcupines inhabit the eastern US from Pennsylvania northward. They, like raccoons, are primarily nocturnal, but unlike raccoons, porcupines are strictly vegetarian. They feed on leaves, twigs, skunk cabbage, clover and lupines in the spring and summer, and in the winter, they chew through the outer bark of trees — firs, pines, cedar or hemlock — to get at the inner bark (*cambium*) which is their staple.

The porcupine's tail and rump are covered by about 30,000

quills, modified hairs, which are solid at the tip and the base, used for defense. When attacked the porcupine lashes with its tail, driving its quills forcefully into its victim. Microscopic barblets at the end of the quills expand and cause the quills to become even more firmly embedded.

DEER

The white-tailed deer is the only small deer on the AT. And for hikers in most states, the only part of the whitetail they will see is the white tail waving as it disappears over a ridge crest.

However, in states with large deer populations — Virginia and Pennsylvania — you are apt to see deer more often and see more of them. In the national parks, deer are almost approachable. It is not uncommon to be able to get within a few yards, if not a few feet, of them. At Silers Bald Shelter in the Smokies, several deer came at dusk to feed on shoots of common plantain growing in the shelter clearing. Some, exhibiting no concern over my presence, approached to within a few feet from where I was sitting.

When aroused or nervous, deer will snort and stamp their feet to alert other deer to danger. Hikers who tent-camp are most likely to hear them during the night.

MOOSE

Moose are the largest deer in the world. The size of a horse, a full grown male can weigh up to 1400 pounds. The body is covered with long, dark, brown hair. A moose's muzzle is very large and pendulous with a large dewlap under the chin. Moose are solitary in the summer but sometimes gather near streams and lakes to feed on aquatic vegetation and willows. They can be found from Vermont north on the Trail. Hikers stand the best chance of seeing moose in Maine where the Trail is filled with moose tracks and scat.

Moose, normally retiring, avoid people. However, they can be unpredictable and dangerous. Cows with calves are fiercely protective. The rut, the mating period between mid-September and late-October, is the bulls' crazy season. Bulls have been known to attack cars and locomotives, as well as people. The surprise when opening a tent flap in the morning to find a moose staring in at you is almost heart-stopping. I had that experience twice. On reflection, having stared a moose in the eye from two or three feet away, I would not describe the animal as intelligent. But what it lacks in brains, it more than makes up for in size, a size that will definitely get one's attention.

ELK

Elk once roamed all through the southern Appalachians, but they have been eliminated from the region because of over hunting and habitat loss. The last elk disappeared from North Carolina as long ago as the end of the 1700's. The mid 1800's saw the last elk in Tennessee and by 1900, the elk population was believed by many to be headed for extinction.

In February, 2001, the NPS introduced two dozen elk into the Smokies and in 2002 and 2003, the Park Service plans to introduce 25-30 animals anually. All elk will be fitted with collars and monitored for the duration of the five-year experimental phase of the project.

It may be possible to see some of these animals as they move through the park, so it is important to realize that these are not overgrown whitetail deer. Elk are much larger than the black bear, and they can be dangerous — particularly females with calves and bulls who may perceive people as challengers to their domain. So, if you are fortunate enough to see an elk, enjoy the viewing but keep your distance.

HARES and RABBITS

Only two species of hares are known to exist along the AT. The most common is the snowshoe hare. Its range is from northern New Jersey northward through Maine. These are seldom seen during periods of low population, except perhaps for the seemingly crazy hares that hang around Greenleaf Hut in the White Mountains.

Primarily vegetarian, unless stealing meat from trap bait, the snowshoe hare eats a wide range of grasses, berries and tree buds.

The snowshoe hare changes colors with the seasons — from dark brown in summer to white in winter. It even changes into motley brown and white during autumn when snow is patchy on the ground.

Hare populations become exceptionally plentiful every nine or ten years, then swiftly plummet. During these periods of high population, hikers have the greatest opportunity to see them. Another hare that may be observed by AT hikers is the brown or European hare that inhabits northern Pennsylvania, eastern New York and western New England up to Vermont. It is larger than the snowshoe hare and does not change colors with the season.

The eastern cottontail and the New England cottontail are the rabbits most likely to be observed. The only really recognizable difference is the black patch between the ears of the New England cottontail. It is also more secretive than the eastern cottontail and rarely ventures from cover, making it unlikely to be seen or recognized by hikers.

SQUIRRELS

The squirrels that hikers can expect to see are the gray squirrel, probably the most common of the squirrels, and also the fox squirrel and the red squirrel. The northern flying squirrel and the southern flying squirrel also inhabit the regions through which the Trail passes, but they are nocturnal and seldom seen.

The gray squirrel, as the name indicates, is gray above with a paler gray underside. In its northern range, it may appear more black. The tail is bushy gray with silver hairs. Nuts, either hickory nuts or acorns, also beech nuts and walnuts, comprise its main diet. The fox squirrel is the largest of the tree squirrels. It has a large bushy tail with yellow-tipped hairs. It has two color phases: in the north, gray with yellowish underside, and in the south, black with white blaze on the face and white tail tip. Its diet is similar to that of the gray squirrel.

The red squirrel inhabits the region of the Trail northward from northern Virginia. It is the smallest tree squirrel, easily recognized by the reddish cast of its coat with white or gray-white underside. Its tail is similar in color but outlined with a broad black band edged in white. It feeds mainly on pine seeds but eats nuts as well. It also feeds on birds' eggs and has been known to eat young birds.

The flying squirrel has loose folds of skin between the front and hind legs which, when extended by the legs, act as a wing enabling the squirrel to glide. The smallest of the squirrels, it is also the most carnivorous, eating in addition to nuts and seeds, insects and sometimes flesh of other small animals.

OPOSSUMS

The Virginia Opossum is the only marsupial species found along the Trail with the exception of Maine. About the size of a large house cat, it is normally grizzled-white above and has long white hairs covering dark fur below. Its most distinguishing feature is its long, naked prehensile tail. The throat and head are whitish. Large, pink-tipped ears are bare of fur.

The opossum is nocturnal and solitary, and it is seldom seen by hikers. It feeds on carrion and many are killed while feeding on road kills. Also, it eats earthworms, snakes, small mammals, insects, frogs, fruits and berries.

SKUNKS

Two species of skunks inhabit the Trail: The spotted skunk and the striped skunk. Hikers are more likely to meet the striped skunk.

The spotted skunk is noticeably smaller than the striped one. Besides size, it differs in that its stripes are horizontal on the neck and shoulders with elongated spots on the sides.

The striped skunk has two broad white stripes running the length of its back and coming together in a cap on the head. From two to just under three feet in length and seven-to-15 inches tall, it weighs up to 14 pounds.

A skunk's defensive weapon is to spray a fetid, oily musk at any attackers. It can direct spray up to 15 feet. The mist can reach three times that far, and the smell may carry a mile.

Carnivores do kill and eat skunks — if they can do so without getting sprayed. However, if confronted by a skunk's threat display, a raised tail, the attacker is likely to retreat. Skunk fluid in the eye is painful and may cause temporary loss of vision. No predator is likely to take that chance.

Skunks are omnivorous and will eat just about anything. That includes people food, and it is not unusual to see skunks foraging around shelters or campgrounds. If confronted by a skunk, back off. Do not chase it with a show of aggression. If it is looking for food, which is all the time, it will scrounge around the shelter or the campsite and usually leave after a few minutes.

Skunks are really fun to watch. They shuffle and waddle as they walk, and when running they are downright ungainly. Their only serious predator is the great-horned owl that can swoop down undetected and carry off young.

No matter how cute or comical, interaction with skunks is discouraged, not just because of their malodorous qualities, but because they are the chief carriers of rabies in America.

WILD TURKEYS

Wild turkeys are found along the Trail from southern Vermont south. Mostly seen in small flocks feeding on the forest floor, they are very wary and will disperse by running for cover through the underbrush at the first detection of a predator.

They feed on berries, acorns, seeds, nuts and insects. The mostly solitary males can grow to four feet tall. The best time to see turkeys is during periods of light rain or mist. Once you see a turkey, because of its size, you will immediately recognize it.

GROUSE

All hikers will encounter ruffed grouse and spruce grouse during a hike of the AT. Ruffed grouse are found in all the states along the Trail. Spruce grouse are found only in Maine.

Grouse are chicken-size birds that feed on seeds, nuts, berries and insects. Ruffed grouse are ground nesters and are as a rule so well camouflaged that one will pass without detecting them unless they take flight. You can look right at a bird and be unaware of its presence until it flushes, which it does with great commotion and which will certainly startle the unwary. The ruffed grouse is normally a mottled red-brown or gray-brown with a brown, banded tail. The spruce grouse is very tame and can be approached to within inches. It is found in the conifer forests in Maine. The males have a black

breast with white barring on the sides. A comb of red skin above the
eyes is visible at close range. The tail has a chestnut band on the tip.

I have passed several of these birds sitting on tree limbs so
close to the Trail that I could have reached out and touched them.

OBSERVING WILDLIFE

The best time to observe wildlife is early in the morning at around
sunrise or in the evening just after sunset. Walk quietly. Be aware
of your surroundings. Stop occasionally to observe the forest. Remain quiet and motionless for 15 minutes or longer. After a few
minutes of silence, the forest will reverberate with sound. You will
be amazed at the amount of animal activity.

Hikers willing to take the time have a unique opportunity to
witness life as nature has shaped it in the wild. However, slowing
down can be difficult for one caught up in the psychological draft
of the power hikers churning toward Katahdin. If there is any question, it is one of personal preference. Is it more important to climb
Katahdin with the first wave or to participate in the wilderness
experience? My personal preference is to experience the wilderness. This is the essence and setting of the adventure.

12

Personal Safety

*"The protected man doesn't need luck;
therefore it seldom visits him."*
Alan Harington

The Appalachian Trail attracts millions of people a year. Naturally, such high numbers of visitors will statistically include troublemakers. Out of every million or so people a certain percentage will be derelicts, defective in character or personality or, sadly, insane. Most of these types never go near the Trail. Occasionally, though, one does, and a tragedy occurs; this happened in 1980 and again in 1990. There have been only six homicides on the AT in its 57-year history. But there have been an increasing number of cases of rape, assault, theft and harassment.

Clearly, the chances of assault occurring on the Trail are much less than in most American cities. Hikers do not assault other hikers, unless partners fall out and a fight occurs.

Serious assaults on hikers are quite rare. However, they do happen — usually in places where hikers come in contact with non-hikers or locals. These events seem to transpire out of some warped sense of "having fun" with the "outsider."

While it is a sad commentary, the age of innocence and trust in one's fellow man — as witnessed when one could leave his home unlocked — has disappeared, not only from town and city, but also from the wilderness, especially the part most accessible to people hiking the AT. There are increasing reports of automobiles stolen or vandalized at Trail heads, or packs and other equipment stolen from hikers as they slept.

The reality is that one must deal with modern life even in a setting as naturally restful as the Appalachian Trail. The protection formerly afforded by culture and "civilization" has broken down. Just as we can no longer walk carefree through parks in our towns, we must also be alert to personal danger on the Trail. Therefore, one should consider actions that will minimize the likelihood of becoming a victim of crime.

Still, in comparison to cities, the AT is very safe. It is only slightly less than 100 percent safe. With this in mind, hikers should take those measures necessary to bring it up to the 100 percent on a personal level. Certain conditions will naturally increase the safety quotient. For example, it is personally safer to hike with a partner than alone. (This is not a guarantee of safety, however.) It is normally safer for males than females. Almost no one will attack someone accompanied by a large dog. In addition to the conditions of safety, a hiker can take a number of measures to enhance personal safety.

Don't trust everybody you meet on the AT. Not everyone on the AT is a hiker. You will sense immediately if someone is a *bonafide* hiker or if they have another reason for being on the Trail. Their demeanor or clothing and equipment tend to be a quick giveaway.

Sometimes drifters or derelicts find their way to the Trail. Usually these people indicate they are coming from Chicago or New York or the West, and that they are passing a few days on the Trail before heading back or on to a job somewhere. Mostly, such stories are enormously interesting — like the guy I met at a shelter in Pennsylvania who was taking a two week vacation from his job as a chef at a large hotel. At first I believed him. Then, he told me he had sutured the leg of a wounded deer with fishing line . . .

When you arrive at a shelter take a close look at the occupants. You will, in all probability, know all the hikers; you will have met them on the Trail. But sometimes you will find only one or two people alone whom you don't know and who don't fit your mental image of hikers. If you feel at all uneasy about the situation, keep on going. If you are hiking with a partner, talk about tactics well before confronting the actual situation.

I have spent a couple of sleepless nights in shelters because of sixth sense concerns about some of the occupants. I later learned my fears were justified. In one instance, two men carried a concealed rifle in their bedroll and killed a deer the following morning after my departure. In another, a young, southbound female hiker posted notes in various shelters south of Monson, Maine, indicating that she was missing several hundred dollars. I had previously stayed at a shelter with her, her younger brother and strange male companion who had triggered my sixth sense. Unexpectedly, about a week later, her male companion appeared in Monson. Coincidence?

Stay clear of shelters near roads or population centers, particularly on weekends. Shelters easily reached by road often become magnets for local party-timers. Drunks are unpredictable. Add to that equation those who think harassing hikers is a sport, and you have a problem. Keep your distance. Pass up those shelters within a mile or a mile and a half of a road. I rarely stayed at shelters in New Jersey, New York or Connecticut simply because they were so accessible.

When you tent camp, select a site that is at least 200 yards off the Trail. At this distance, unless you snore very loudly, your presence is likely to go undetected except for raccoons or deer.

In talking to strangers, keep the details of your itinerary to yourself. If you are alone, mention that others are behind you. Don't offer any information about where you plan to spend the night.

If you are already at a shelter, and someone arrives who makes you feel uncomfortable, move on — no matter how tired you are or how bad the weather. Sixth senses are important. Rely on them. A good dose of healthy skepticism is an important ingredient in maintaining safety.

If any incidents should occur, report them to the local authorities and the ATC. Seemingly unimportant pieces of information, when pieced together, often create a full and clear picture.

The question often arises, "Did you carry a gun?" No thru-hiker I knew carried a gun. Perhaps some did, but guns are not allowed in national parks. In the hands of people unfamiliar with handling weapons, guns can be dangerous. Also, many hikers are outraged by the thought of people violating the ideological sanctity of the AT by carrying a gun. To them, the AT is a place of natural peace and tranquility, and the introduction of weapons onto the AT destroys the natural harmony. Their position basically states that if you feel it is necessary to carry a gun, you don't understand what the AT is all about. I agree with their philosophy. However, philosophy sometimes fails to identify with reality.

I know that some people on the AT belong to the one-tenth of one percent of the population that includes the mentally or spiritually deficient. These people have no concept of idealism in their personal lives and are ignorant of the philosophy governing the idealism of believers in the AT. It is only provident to be capable of self-defense in the event of an assault from one of these predators. A firearm is a powerful deterrent or, if deterrence fails, is a powerful defense against someone believing he has received a divine message to take your life.

I wonder if the couple murdered at Wapiti Shelter in Virginia in 1980 or if Geoff Hood or Molly LaRue, murdered in Pennsylvania in 1990, would be alive today if one of them had carried a pistol for self-defense. I know that on a couple of occasions my partner and I felt more secure, knowing that if a situation developed into extreme danger, I had the capability for self-defense.

Firearms in the hands of someone morally responsible, knowledgeable and practiced in their use are not a problem. Firearms in the hands of irresponsible, untrained or immature people are a menace. It is important that those who consider it necessary to carry a firearm, understand and respect the power and destructiveness of a gun. In addition, they should be completely knowledgeable about how to handle and use it.

They should also be sure to understand the "rules of engagement," i. e., when the use of a gun is justified. These decisions are not easily arrived at or recognized at the time the decision is needed. Few people are psychologically equipped to deal with that reality.

In the final analysis, the best advice is to leave the gun at home. Statistics do not warrant carrying a firearm, and you can use the weight for something more constructive.

While dogs can enhance a hiker's security on the Trail, they introduce another set of unique problems. Dogs have to be trained, fed and cared for. They must also learn that every shelter where they spend the night does not become personal territory to be defended to the death.

There are also severe bureaucratic drawbacks to hiking with a dog. On all lands under the administration of the National Park Service, dogs must be kept on a leash. This includes about 40% of the AT. It also includes the Blue Ridge Parkway, Shenandoah National Park, the Harpers Ferry and C&O Canal national historic parks and the Delaware Water Gap National Recreational area. Dogs are not allowed at all in the Great Smoky Mountains National Park.

Dogs are also not allowed in the Trailside Museums and Wildlife center section of Bear Mountain State Park in New York. Hikers with dogs or those hiking through this area during nonbusiness hours can take the alternate route along Route 9W or cross Route 9W to Hessian Lake. Dogs are also not permitted in Baxter State Park in Maine.

These restrictions present considerable obstacles to those hiking with dogs. Owners must arrange not only for their dog's care when traversing dog-restricted areas but also times and points for rendez-vous after crossing those areas.

Additional drawbacks must be considered. If you are accompanied by a dog, it is almost axiomatic that you will see few wild animals. Most other hikers prefer not to hike with someone with a dog. Some owners allow their dogs to bother other hikers by begging for food. Now and then, a wet dog will walk over other hikers' equipment in a shelter, muddying sleeping bags and other gear. Dogs have no priority for space in a shelter. Dogs chasing into the night every time a squirrel or a raccoon blunders into the area disrupt others who are sleeping.

Dogs, like people, become tired and injured. More than one dog has died from overheating or overexertion. Also, dogs require food and water which someone has to carry. Many dogs are fitted with saddlebags that carry their food. But if a dog is overloaded, this may lead to injury.

Again, the decision to bring a dog onto the Trail is a highly personal one. Just as with guns, there are good arguments on both sides of the question. Certainly, the dog must be in good physical condition. It must be well-trained, and under positive and instant control at all times. If unable to meet these requirements, one should not bring a dog on the Trail.

There are times when hikers must leave the Trail to resupply or pick up a mail drop. At these times, hikers are most vulnerable to assault or harassment. This may be reduced by timing. It is better to go into a town during weekdays than on weekends. It is preferable to go early in the day and certainly not after dark. Do not accept rides unless you are comfortable with the people making the offer. A ride from a 70-year-old lady in a 1960 Buick is safer than one from a pair of long-haired, beer-swilling young men sporting tattoos and driving a battered pickup truck.

To reduce exposure time, stash and hide your pack before heading into town. There are going to be places, like in Maine, where a quick hike is impractical. Some distances are more than ten miles one way. In that case, plan on hiking the road the whole day — unless you are willing to hitchhike.

However, hitchhiking in remote areas like Maine is not nearly the problem it is in more heavily populated areas. People in Maine and New Hampshire are unusually friendly, and those who drive the roads crossed by the Trail often see hikers bouncing down the road; these folks are likely to offer a lift into town.

Safety on the Trail is an important consideration to a successful and enjoyable hike. Stay alert, just as you would at home in the city. Be aware that although the Trail is a very safe environment, one will occasionally meet less than desirable people. Plan and act accordingly — and enhance your personal safety.

I have mentioned earlier that hikers need not fear any animals on the Trail. Domestic dogs are an exception. Most are not a problem. They will simply bark you off their turf. Sometimes, though, a hiker will meet a dangerous dog.

I remember several instances of hikers being attacked by a dog in New Hampshire. Notes in shelter registers in the vicinity warned hikers about the animal. Even so, Tom Gertsma (G-Man), whom I encountered occasionally during my hike, had been bitten. He did not carry a hiking stick. He described the attack: A man was standing on the porch of his house watching the attack. G-Man yelled at the man to call off the dog. The man ignored his pleas and went inside the house leaving the dog to continue the attack.

I was attacked by two dogs, a golden labrador retriever and a Doberman pincer on the road (the AT at the time) into Linden, VA. The dogs both came from a house adjacent to the road. I yelled repeatedly, trying to get someone in the house to respond. No one responded. Fortunately, I carried my hiking stick. By using it and backing down the road until I was out of their territory, I was able to escape injury. My heart was still fluttering 30 minutes later when I reached the little general store on Route 55. Had I not had a hiking stick, I'm sure I would have been bitten.

There were other instances when just the sight of my stick was sufficient to dissuade a dog from doing anything but bark. I know of no one carrying a stick who was bitten by a dog. Hiking sticks have many uses, but dog intimidation is, for me, the primary one.

Sanitation

*"What separates two people most profoundly is
a different sense and degree of cleanliness."*
Nietzsche

Sanitation on the Trail falls into three categories: personal cleanliness, disposal of waste, and cleanliness of food utensils.

Personal cleanliness is simply a matter of discipline, of taking the time and effort to keep clean. On the Trail, the body accumulates dirt quickly. A couple of hours of climbing and rock scrambling produces prodigious amounts of sweat and grime that seem to accumulate exponentially each day one does not bathe.

A steaming hot shower assumes the aura of luxury. Its unavailability makes it the stuff from which dreams are made. Since there are no hot showers or tubs of water waiting for the hiker at day's end, how does one stay clean in the wilderness?

Sponge bathing in cold water from a canteen is the answer. It is not like a hot shower, but it is often the only way to bathe, and it is effective. Use biodegradable soap and do it well away, at least 150 feet, from water sources such as springs or streams. Pour dirty water onto the soil. If a pond or lake is accessible, after rinsing off, a cool dip can be refreshing. The market offers many brands of biodegradable soap. I used Dr. Bronner's Peppermint 18-in-1 Pure

Castile Soap. It worked well, although the peppermint caused very tingly sensations on the more sensitive parts of my body. Actually, Dr. Bronner's label is worth the cost of the soap. One extract follows: "Enjoy the creamy emollient lather on baby, bath, beach, body, dentures, mint deodorant, shaving, mouthwash-silk-wool-pets-rugs-diapers-car-hand & foot soap." Some do not think it works very well as hair shampoo.

Another soap, Trak, an all-purpose cleanser, meets general soap requirements, as well as being a good hair shampoo. This comes in a plastic tube, which makes it easy to handle. Other brands include Camp Suds, Bio Suds, Mountain Suds and Paket. Most camping equipment stores carry these and other brands.

A towel is optional, a wash cloth unnecessary. I carried a small kitchen towel, and if for some reason it was wet, I dried myself with a bandanna or a sock that I subsequently hung from my pack to dry.

Deodorant is also optional. After a day or two on the Trail, a hiker is going to smell. After several days, one will reek. In the wild, around others with similar odoriferous impairment, no one cares. For visits to civilization, however, a little dab of deodorant increases the chance of acceptance. For that reason, I carried a small plastic bottle of Arid.

For dental care, a small toothbrush, a small tube of toothpaste and a roll of dental floss will suffice. Some purists suggest cutting off half of the toothbrush handle and boring holes in the remainder to reduce weight. Some think that is ludicrous. When rinsing the mouth, do so away from water sources, preferably directly on soil.

Freeman Industries, the maker of Trak, also offers Mini-Trak Kit, a backpacker toiletry kit consisting of a small tube of Trak soap, a vial of dentifrice, a folding toothbrush, and a paper towel — all for under $5.

A small comb is advisable when a hiker goes to town, as in Damascus, Virginia, Hot Springs, North Carolina, and Monson, Maine.

Some men carried razors. Most didn't. I don't know if women carried razors in their toilet kits. But I grew a beard for the first time in my life at age 52 on the Trail, and it is still with me, albeit slightly grayer. One firm, EMS, offers a battery-powered electric razor for those who simply must shave. It weighs five ounces without the battery and costs about $15. For other than signaling purposes, a mirror is really superfluous unless looking good is a very high priority. But be warned. After a few days on the Trail, your mirror image may be enough to make you bury the thing in the bottom of your pack.

Personal hygiene is just that, personal, and except for protecting water sources, affects only the individual. Disposal of body waste is another story. With the proliferation of hikers on the AT comes also a proliferation in threats to the environment.

Flush toilets with sewers leading to water treatment plants do not exist in the wilderness. Each hiker must understand this and be aware that raw body waste has great potential to pollute and affect others. Hikers *must* dispose of their waste safely with minimum impact on the environment.

To assist hikers, Trail clubs have constructed many privies in the vicinity of shelters, and hikers are encouraged to use them. Unfortunately, all shelters — the majority, in fact — do not have privies. The ATC recognizes this shortcoming and has adopted a policy of providing a privy at every shelter. However, getting independent hiking clubs to install privies is more difficult than establishing policy. Building privies is not nearly as glamorous as building a shelter. Still, great progress has been made. Privies have been built at several shelters in the Smokies and at other locations as well.

In Vermont, at least one camp site has a composting privy where waste is mixed with wood shavings and dried in solar heated bins. After treatment, shavings can be reused or returned to the environment.

Very likely, a privy will not be available when a hiker needs it most. What to do? There is a right and a wrong way to handle the problem. Many roadside pull-offs provide numerous examples of the wrong way. If done properly, there will be little or no evidence, and the environment will not be affected.

Now for the right way . . . First, select a site that is at least 150 feet from any water course, the farther away the better. The ground must be soft enough to dig a hole to bury the waste. Rocky sites are unacceptable. Second, dig a "cat" hole, at least five or six inches deep, preferably deeper. Deposit the feces. If possible, burn the toilet paper and place the residue in the hole. If burning is not possible, simply place the toilet paper in the hole. Fill the hole with soil. The soil will act as a natural filter; over time, bacterial action and filtration will cleanse the waste. It is important to get the feces under soil to remove it as an attraction to flies.

Be sensible about the location of your private john. Avoid places where others are likely to camp. Carry a small plastic trowel for digging. Trowels can be purchased in any camp store and in most hardware stores for about a dollar. They can also be ordered from catalogues.

Urination does not present nearly the problem of defecation. The prudent urinate in soil away from water sources. Those who need to urinate frequently during the night might consider carrying a wide-mouthed plastic bottle with a cap for surreptitious use in a shelter or tent.

Cleanliness of cooking utensils is also important to maintaining good health on the Trail. Dr. Bronner's Pure-Castile soap worked perfectly well as a dish washing soap for pots and utensils. Rinse thoroughly. Hot water and a plastic scrub pad will easily remove food scraps prior to washing.

Clean pots and utensils away from water sources. Nothing irritates hikers more than seeing the remains of someone's meal in a stream or at the base of a spring.

Clothes need periodic laundering. Different people have different personal body odors and grunge tolerances, so the frequency of washing fluctuates according to individual endurance. I could endure my shirt for five days and my pants for ten. Socks lasted three days maximum.

I carried no soap powder or detergent, relying instead on soap dispensing machines at laundromats. It was expensive and often aggravating, especially acquiring sufficient coins to pay for laundry detergent. The alternative of carrying detergent with me was not an option, since it was just one more item to carry on my back.

Instead I carried a plastic laundry bag (heavy duty trash bag) in my pack. When an item became too filthy, I placed it in the laundry bag. When the bag was full or when I ran out of clean clothes, I headed for the laundromat. Sanitation on the Trail requires effort and common sense. Every hiker must realize he or she shares the Trail with many others. Consideration of others and the environment is essential.

When every hiker observes the rules of sanitation, the result is enjoyment and appreciation of the resource by all. However, only one careless or thoughtless act can foul a beautiful setting. The effect is immediate and often degrades the experience for many other hikers. Also, when a single person abuses the environment, there is a tendency for others to contribute to the desecration. One of the most attractive characteristics of the AT is that almost all hikers observe the rules.

14

Trail Etiquette

"Manners are the happy ways of doing things;
each once a stroke of genius or of love, now
repeated and hardened into usage."
Emerson

One of the appealing aspects of hiking in general and the Appalachian Trail in particular — there is no written body of rules or laws governing hiking. Of course, if there were any — the Trail in most instances is usually remote — such rules would be difficult to enforce.

This absence of written rules does not imply an absence of moral or ethical imperatives, however. To the contrary. Because the Trail is often remote does not mean its environment is secure. Even in seldom visited areas, ecological balances and the environment can be damaged by carelessness or ignorance. For this reason, certain usage "rules" have evolved to protect the Appalachian Trail and its environment for future visitors. Although usage guides are important for sparsely populated regions, they are absolutely essential where population impact is severe. The Trail corridors adjacent to population centers in Pennsylvania, New Jersey, New York and Connecticut etc., and, of course, in national and state parks — where heavy usage occurs — come immediately to mind as needing the most care. Backwoods usage "rules" are effective only when people understand the reasons for them and are willing to observe them on the "honor system." Individual responsibility is the key ingredient for success. It is essential.

No authority figure will arrest anybody failing to follow a "rule." But those who break the hiker's code, so to speak, must deal with their consciences and are often censured by their peers. This does not mean that violations are rare. Everyday the hiker will encounter evidence that bears witness to violations. Mainly, these are the result of ignorance.

Therefore, it is incumbent for those entering the wilderness to educate themselves about the realm visited. It is imperative to learn that we are visitors, not conquerors or civilizers. Thru-hikers, especially, must learn to function as one with the natural world through which they are passing. This is the only way to protect the wilderness. It is called "low-impact hiking."

The saying, "Take nothing but photographs and leave nothing but footprints," sums up neatly the basic philosophy of low-impact hiking. One's presence in wilderness should be transitory. No record or traces of the presence should remain after one's departure.

Leave no litter. Carry out all plastic and paper wrappers. This applies to even insignificant items like cellophane candy wrappers or cigarette filter tips. Pack out organic trash — for instance, orange peels take months to decompose. Do not attempt to burn aluminum foil packets. (These account for most unsightly conditions at shelter fire pits.) Carry them out. Carry out all cans. If you encounter trash on the Trail and you have the capability, pack it out. The concept of low-impact hiking is doing your part and then some.

Do not start fires. Use your camp stove for cooking. Leave the saw and hatchet at home. If you feel a fire is a must, under no circumstances cut live trees; use only downed wood. Because of increased Trail usage, it is becoming more difficult to find downed wood in the vicinity of shelters. Certainly, use only fire pits for fires and keep them small. Do not burn or leave trash in a fire pit. Of all the backwoods "rules" violations I have observed on the Trail, this was the most frequent one — burning or leaving trash in a fire pit.

As I have indicated, properly dispose of all body waste. Nothing is more aesthetically disturbing than toilet paper and human feces in an otherwise pristine environment. And nothing can be more hygienically threatening to the environment or the health of others. When walking, stay on the Trail. Bypassing switchbacks causes trail erosion. Countless violations of this "rule" can be seen throughout the Trail. If the path is not wide enough to accommodate two hikers side-by-side, then walk Indian file rather than skirt the trail edge and widen it.

Keep the number of members in your hiking party to under ten. The fewer the better. Experience indicates that visits by large groups have a far greater impact on the environment than visits by the same number of people spaced out over time. Large groups require more space and the impact of their presence is broader. Take rest breaks only in places where your presence will not damage vegetation.

Leave the wildflowers alone. In fact, leave all vegetation alone. Others should have the same opportunity to admire vegetation as you have. If you feel you must carry their beauty with you, do it with a photograph.

Foraging for wild edibles is likewise discouraged. You do not need it for survival or even passing nutrition. Leave it for the animals or for others to see. Especially plump and tempting blackberries are exceptions to this rule!

Above treeline, the Alpine vegetation is especially fragile. Under no circumstances should one leave the Trail in these locations, particularly because so few Alpine areas exist. (The White Mountains and perhaps a few selected other places in New Hampshire and Maine.) In the White Mountains near Lakes of the Clouds Hut and just below Mt. Washington, a rare Alpine cinquefoil (flowering plant) is found. Signs admonish hikers to stay on the pathway.

Camp in designated camp sites or well away from the Trail — 150 feet or more. Stay at least 150 feet from water sources. (Half the length of a football field.) Select tent sites that do not require trenching for drainage. Some people even suggest selecting tent fabric colors that blend with the environment, greens and browns, as opposed to fluorescent reds and yellows that clash with the natural setting.

Wash bodies and utensils with biodegradable soap well away from water sources. Do not bury food scraps. Any number of critters will tear up the countryside in search of them. Pack unused food out.

If you are accompanied by a dog, keep it under control. Do not let it annoy other hikers by walking over their equipment in shelters or begging for food. Dogs have no priority for space in a shelter. Do not allow the dog to relieve itself around the shelter.

During periods of bad weather, no matter how crowded it may seem, there is always room for one more in the shelter.

When hiking, remember that common courtesy and common sense are the order of the day. The pathway is the result of intense volunteer effort by many people to provide a resource for all to use. There are no charges or fees for hiking. However, anything you do to correct a problem or improve a situation is considered part payment for the benefits and privileges you enjoy. If you have the time, take a few minutes to repair a damaged pathway.

Improving drainage of the Trail is often a simple matter of clearing a water bar. The water bars, usually logs laid diagonally in the path, guide water down over the side of the Trail. Sometimes these fill with dirt or debris that limits their function. Many times, simply scraping the uphill side of the bar with a boot heel will allow water to flow properly.

Block off "volunteer trails," bypasses of switchbacks, when possible. Bypasses can lead to severe erosion of the pathway. Obviously, one hiker cannot fix every "volunteer trail" encountered, but repairing just one a week helps. Consider, if every hiker fixed just one bypass a week, and none created any more, the problem would go away.

One of the primary reasons, other than ignorance, for violations of backwoods "rules" is fatigue. It can sometimes be onerous to leave a water source while bathing or to bypass an attractive camp site near the water for one that is less aesthetically pleasing farther into the woods. But we all must think about the impact of our actions on the environment and of the legacy we leave for those who follow.

In reality, low-impact hiking is not a set of cold, impersonal rules promulgated by government. It is a concept of living. It is living in harmony with the wilderness. It is respecting the environment and hiking in a way that reflects this respect. It is acknowledgment that we are stewards of an irreplaceable natural world, and how we exercise our stewardship will impact on our children for generations to come. To this point, our record is spotty. We must do better. In essence, it is up to you and me!

On the Trail

"He who travels much, knows much."
Thomas Fuller, MD

FINANCES

By most estimates, a good financial figure for planning a thru-hike is about $2,000, not counting equipment costs. It can be done for less and certainly, for those wishing to indulge in periodic overnights in motels, occasional dining in restaurants and modest amounts ice cream and beer, the cost can be much higher. I did not keep an exact tally of my expenses, but I am sure it was not significantly more than the $2,000 figure, and I took every opportunity to enjoy comfort.

Access to money can be a problem. Starting off from Springer Mountain, Georgia, with a $2,000 wad of bills in one's pocket is not the most efficient nor the safest way to access funds. Most thru-hikers carry travellers checks and replenish as needed at mail drops. Small denominations ($20) are better than large ones ($50 or $100), since mom-and-pop general stores often do not have sufficient money on hand to make change for large bills. As with currency, carrying a large supply of travellers checks is also not wise. Periodic replenishment is preferable.

Another technique — one I used almost exclusively — is to

secure cash advances on credit cards such as MasterCard and VISA or bank debit cards. I normally secured about $200 at a time which was usually more than adequate for two weeks, depending on the availability of ice cream and beer, and the number of restaurants located near the Trail.

It is provident to carry a credit card in the event a major piece of equipment needs replacement or an emergency arises requiring a car rental, air fare or a visit to a doctor.

NAVIGATION

The AT is marked approximately every 100 yards with white blazes, single white paint stripes about six inches long and two inches wide, conspicuously painted on trees or rocks. Changes in Trail direction are marked with two white blazes, one above the other. Approaches to the AT or side trails are marked with light blue blazes.

The Trail is so well marked, it almost requires a deliberate effort to get lost. Occasionally, when fog or mist settles and visibility is reduced, it may be difficult to locate the next blaze. The problem does not arise in the forest where the pathway is always well defined. It arises when crossing large fields, pastures or balds, where one cannot see the far side of the field, and the path is indistinct.

During such periods, I found that dead reckoning generally kept me heading in the right direction. I simply walked an imaginary line from where the Trail emerged from the forest to where I anticipated finding the next blaze. I was successful about 90 percent of the time. If I failed to locate a blaze, I walked along the treeline until I ran into it. Once or twice I had to crisscross the forest edge until I located a blaze.

Occasionally, one may miss a turn. That happened several times. Mostly, it results from not paying attention to the Trail markings. If one observes no blazes after walking for several hundred yards, turn around and go back to the last blaze. Then, start paying attention.

Maps can be purchased with Trail Guides. The quality of these maps varies somewhat because they are prepared by the various trail clubs, but they are all more than adequate for navigating The Trail. One excellent feature of the maps is that all have trail profiles measured against mileage scales which depict various elevations, and the steepness of ascents and descents.

Some thru-hikers carry no maps or guidebooks. They simply follow the white blazes. This is perfectly acceptable for those focused on power hiking with little time or interest in the other dynamics of hiking. A compass is irrelevant. At no time did I feel any limitations because I lacked one. However, if one did become lost in a place like the Maine woods, a compass would indeed be very valuable.

The *Trail Guides* contain detailed Trail descriptions by section and information, such as road approaches, points of interest, general descriptions of each section, shelters and campsites, supplies, services and accommodations, government regulations and sometimes historical information.

All thru-hikers should at least carry the *Trail Guide* pertaining to the section or state they are hiking. Again, it is inefficient to carry all 12 *Trail Guides* from the beginning of one's hike. I carried only two *Trail Guides* and their accompanying maps — one for the state or section I was hiking, and one for the next state or section. I secured new *Trail Guides* from postal drops and at the same time mailed the old ones home.

Generally, by the time I finished with a *Trail Guide*, it was in tatters. I referred to them continually, and the simple wear and tear of taking them out of and putting them into my pocket as well as exposing them to moisture, perspiration or rain caused rapid deterioration. Placing them in a Ziploc bag helped extend book life.

WEATHER

Trying to determine what to expect from the weather can be difficult. But by careful observation, the behavior of animals and insects will give indications of changes in the weather.

For example, the old rhyme, "Red sky at night, a sailor's delight; red sky in the morning, a sailor's warning," is a good indicator of coming weather. A red sky in the evening indicates little moisture in the atmosphere. Conversely, a red sky or red sun in the morning suggests that a storm is approaching.

Hawks or other raptors increase their circling when a storm is approaching. They are watching for mice or other small prey making preparations for an oncoming storm.

When storms are approaching insects, avoiding turbulent air, stay closer to the ground, thus inviting birds to feed closer to the ground. If the birds are feeding higher in the air, it is an indication of good weather.

If bees disappear suddenly, storm activity is imminent. Of course, one will usually hear thunder by that time. The tree leaves of the hardwoods will turn bottom side up — anywhere from 12-to-24 hours before a storm. Increases in wind velocity closer to the earth are usually harbingers of an approaching storm. The sounds of grouse drumming, or car horns or train whistles become clearer when increased moisture in the air indicates the possibility of a storm. Mists rising from valleys in the morning means fair weather. Conversely, if mists settle in the morning and rise in the evening, bad weather may be approaching.

Morning glories open in fair weather and close in anticipation of rain. These and many other indicators of future or near-term weather can help hikers anticipate the weather. Of course, how one reacts to the weather is the real issue.

Prepare for rain before it arrives. Place such things as toilet paper, maps, *Trail Guides*, matches and paper in Ziploc bags. Stuff sleeping bags in plastic garbage bags before placing in stuff sacks. Before turning in, bring all weather-affected gear inside the tent or shelter or protect it with a water proof cover.

INSECT PROTECTION

Bugs: Mosquitoes, no-see-ums, gnats, fleas, black flies and a host of blood suckers are constant companions on the Trail. They can be minor irritations or major problems, depending on time of year and location. Black fly season is a summer phenomenon in the far north. They are not a problem in the south. Mosquitoes are a menace around water and in the evening. During the day and in sunlight, they are less of a problem. Gnats are a total pain in hot weather in the forests of the south. For some reason, an open eye is irresistible to them. No-see-ums join the mosquitoes around dusk and can be a source of major discomfort. You can't see the critters, so they attack with impunity.

In some places in the south, white-faced hornets seem unduly attracted to hikers. They usually do not sting. I use the word "usually" instead of "never." Although I have not been stung and know of no one who has, they can sting, and I can imagine somewhere in the past someone has been stung. Just ignore them and be careful when donning your pack that one is not trapped under the harness.

What to do for protection? Most try insect repellant, and for most it works quite well. Insect repellants contain DEET (N,N-Di-ethyl-meta-toluamide). The more effective repellants contain higher concentrations of DEET.

Some people recommend Avon's Skin-So-Soft as a repellant, but I was not impressed. For me, repellants with DEET worked better. DEET is more effective, since it masks body odor, creates a smell that confuses insect receptors and produces an oily film disagreeable to insects. But for some, particularly those sensitive to DEET, its use can be a problem. When the skin becomes heated, pores open for perspiration — allowing absorption of the DEET. Also, perspiration dilutes DEET, and it must be periodically reapplied. Repeated applications of repellant with substantial quantities of DEET can cause uncomfortable reactions even for those with not especially sensitive skin.

Some people solve this problem by applying repellant to clothing. This can be effective in light concentrations of insects but may not work in places where insects swarm. In this case, it may be necessary to use gloves, face netting and long pants to protect exposed skin — not very attractive in hot weather — but it will do the job.

Muskol is widely recognized as the most effective repellant. It contains about 95 percent DEET. Repel 100, containing about the same amount of DEET, is also good. Repel Standard contains around 52 percent DEET and is good, but not as good as the others. Then, of course, there are the standard super market brands, OFF! and others that work fine on the back yard patio, but not as well in the forest.

A few new organic-based repellants have been developed and are now available commercially. These products consist of combinations of natural substances that were known for their bug repellant properties before DEET was developed. In most cases it will be necessary to apply more of the product more often than DEET to obtain the same protection. No known side effects of these new products have been discovered. These are very new to the market and have not been subjected to long periods of independent testing. But they are very promising and worthy of hiker confidence:

- *Repel Lemon Eucalyptus* — Ingredients mostly lemon oil and eucalyptus. Tests found the greasy, white formula to be effective for up to eight hours. Available through WPC Brands, Inc., phone (800) 558-6614 or visit the website: http://www.destinationoutdoors.com.

- *Badger Anti-Bug Balm* — Consists mostly of essential oil of eucalyptus citridora, beeswax, castor oil and extra virgin olive oil. Works
  for up to four hours. From W.S. Badger Co., Inc., phone (800) 603-
  6100, or visit the website: http://www.badgerbalm.com.
- *Natrapel* — Mainly citronella. Spray or lotion. Not greasy. Effective for up to two hours. From Tender Corp., phone (800) 258-4649,
  or visit the website: http://www.tendercorp.com.
- *Green Ban* — Has cajeput, myrth, citronella, galbanum, lavender
  and peppermint. Lasts for up to four hours. From Kokopelli Dis-
  tributors, phone (303) 469-9510, or visit the website: http://
  www.greenban.com.
- *Cactus Juice Insect Protection* — Smells like oranges and contains
  SPF sunscreen. Not greasy. Repels insects for six hours. From Safe
  Solutions, Inc., phone (877) 554-5222, or visit the website: http://
  www.cactusjuicetm.com.

GETTING TO THE TRAIL

For those beginning at Springer Mountain, Georgia, there are basically
three approaches. The one, from the south, is from Amicalola Falls
State Park. A second, also from the south, is from Nimblewill Gap,
and the third, from the north, is a forest service road.

Of all the approaches, the one from Amicalola Falls State Park is
the longest and the most difficult. One major advantage, however, is
the availability of parking and other facilities. This advantage is offset
by the distance to be covered — 11 miles over some rough and, occasionally, very steep terrain. It can take the uninitiated two days of
hiking just to reach their start point on Springer Mountain. There are
reports of prospective thru-hikers being so impacted by the difficulty
of the climb up Amicalola Mountain that they aborted their adventure
even before reaching the start-point.

The blue-blazed approach trail from Amicalola State Park to
Springer Mountain passes through Nimblewill Gap. The Gap can be
reached by road and a spacious turn around area for vehicles facilitates
using this as a drop off point for beginners. To reach the Gap take
Georgia Route 9 north of Dawsonville. Turn left onto Georgia Route
52. After four miles (old store), turn right. After 6.6 miles come to
Nimblewill Church and road on left where pavement ends. Continue

for 14 miles over rough, winding mountain road to Nimblewill Gap. The blue-blaze trail to the right leads 2.3 miles to Springer Mountain.

To approach Springer Mountain from the north, take the all-weather unpaved road southwest from Suches to Hightower Gap, about 12.7 miles. At Hightower Gap, follow Forest Service (FS) Road 42 for 3.9 miles to Winding Stair Gap. Several side roads meet FS Road 42 in this gap. Continue straight ahead on FS Road 42 for 1 mile to Big Stamp Gap and then for another 1.3 miles to where the AT crosses the road. It is .9 miles left/south to the summit of Springer Mountain. An open field to the south side of the road provides parking space.

For those beginning at Katahdin, many simply follow the Appalachian Trail itself (also known as the Hunt Trail) from Katahdin Stream Campground to Baxter Peak, the highest summit on Katahdin, also the highest mountain in Maine (5,267 ft.) and the northern terminus of the Trail. Most do this with light packs during good weather. Unfavorable weather can be dangerous on Katahdin, particularly above the treeline along Hunt Spur. In this case, delay the hike until weather allows. Weather forecasts are posted on the bulletin boards of the campgrounds.

An alternate route is the Abol Trail from the Abol Campground up the Abol Slide to Thoreau Spring and thence along Hunt Spur to Baxter Peak. Two other approaches both begin at Roaring Brook Campgound. One leads to the campsite at Chimney Pond in the Great Basin, then follows Cathedral Trail to Baxter Peak. Another, the Helon Taylor Trail, leads to Chimney Peak, then along the Knife Edge to Baxter Peak.

Katahdin is more difficult to reach than Springer Mountain; it lies in the middle of a large state wilderness park with few road approaches and limited access once inside the park. Millinocket, Maine, is the main point of departure for Katahdin. From Millinocket, it is 16 miles via Baxter Park Road along Millinocket Lake to the point where the road turns right for the Park's Togue Pond Gate entrance. From here, it is another 8.2 miles to Katahdin Stream Campground or 12 miles to Daicey Pond Campground.

HINTS

About 30 miles from Springer Mountain to Neels Gap and the Mountain Crossings is Walasi-yi Center, where Dorothy and Jeff Hansen have created a first class hiking equipment business. If one experiences equipment problems or failures, the Mountain Crossings is ideally situated to help with the problem. Dorothy is a former end-to-end thru-hiker, and there isn't much she doesn't know about the Trail and hiking equipment.

When walking, find a pace that's comfortable and stick with it. During climbs, take small steps initially and straighten the legs out with each step. It is less tiring than trying to cover too much ground with large steps.

Carry a small notebook or trail journal to record the important events in your hike. I wrote about everything I saw, how I felt, what thoughts went through my mind, the people I met, animals, wild flowers and photographs I took. I summarized my experiences, and my journals became the basis for my books, *The Appalachian Trail: A Journey of Discovery* and *The Appalachian Trail: Onward to Katahdin*.

Give yourself a Trail name. This is a tradition; although it may seem silly at first, it is the name others remember. You will be known throughout the Trail community by your Trail name. In fact, if you introduce yourself by your given name, you will probably not be recognized, but if you introduce yourself by your Trail name, you will receive instant and universally friendly recognition.

Always take a few minutes to read the Trail registers and to leave note of your passing. You will learn a great deal about your fellow hikers. Most sign off with their trail names. Some entries contain advice or caution that is invaluable to other hikers. Some hikers leave personal messages for those following or just tell about experiences. Some contain humorous anecdotes that would make Dave Barry envious. Others contain marvelous pen-and-ink drawings or caricatures created by talented artists.

A useful guide is Dan Bruce's, *The Thru-Hiker's Handbook: #1 Guide for Long Distance Hikes on the Appalachian Trail . . . with town maps and mileage data from Georgia to Maine*. This book is loaded with helpful hints and energy and time-saving information. Dan updates this book yearly with input from recent thru-hikers. I highly recommend carrying a copy along on your hike. It is also available by mail order through the ATC's "Ultimate Trail Store."

Even the most dedicated thru-hikers will suffer periods of doubt about staying on the Trail. When your turn comes, don't be afraid to get off the Trail for a day or two, indulge yourself, then head back to the Trail. You will be glad you continued on with this adventure of a lifetime!

16

Special Hikes Along the AT

"My heart is warm with friends I make,
And better friends I'll not be knowing;
Yet there isn't a train I wouldn't take,
No matter where it's going."
Edna St. Vincent Millay

Few people can put their families and jobs on hold for five or six months to thru-hike the AT. For them, thru-hiking is a somewhat distant dream, visited occasionally in fantasy or in reality only on weekends or during annual vacations. For this vast majority of hikers, the only contact with wilderness is an occasional visit to a national park or a day-hike along a local nature trail. For those willing to invest a little more time, certain sections of the Appalachian Trail offer exciting possibilities to enjoy the beauty and solitude of a wilderness experience. What follows will provide some insight to certain parts of the Trail and guide you to making the most of the short time you may have in pursuit of your dream.

The task of finding solitude or pristine wilderness anywhere is becoming increasingly more difficult. The Trail is no exception. In some places, particularly, New York, New Jersey, Connecticut and to a lesser degree, Pennsylvania and Massachusetts, the Trail is surrounded by fairly dense development. Although with superhuman effort, the ATC and the Trail Clubs have managed to get the Trail off roads, still, the press of urbanization is difficult to escape. Yet, some truly inspiring stretches of the Trail are not too distant from population centers.

WHITE MOUNTAINS

Probably the section of the Trail most noted for natural splendor and grandeur is the one encompassing the White Mountains in New Hampshire. This is in a class by itself. Obviously, such natural beauty easily accessible to the population centers of New England will scarcely provide solitude.

To the contrary, during the summer season, if one expects to stay at any of the facilities run by the Appalachian Mountain Club (AMC) in the White Mountains, reservations are mandatory. The Trails are filled with people and the huts are always full. Yet, the terrain is spectacular. Replete with fragile Alpine meadows, jagged rock formations and 360 degrees of spectacular vistas, the White Mountains offer truly inspiring natural grandeur.

The Presidential Range with Mount Washington at the center and surrounded by a chain of peaks including Mounts Adams, Eisenhower, Monroe and others are all several thousand feet above treeline with typically barren rock fields and occasional glacial ponds and waterfalls. Numerous side trails offer visitors access to almost all of the range.

Approaches to the Trail can be found in all the main valleys, most notably Kinsman Notch, Crawford Notch, Franconia Notch and Pinkham Notch. And although the Trails are heavily used, relatively few people stray very far from the tourist attractions that defile Franconia Notch and other access points. Most of the people one meets at the huts and along the Trail have expended considerable energy and expense to get there. They universally appreciate the beauty and are considerate of the environment and their neighbors.

Anyone planning to stay at the AMC Huts in the White Mountains should bring lots of money. Bed and breakfast at the huts for nonmembers in 1994-95 cost $47 per night, bed and supper cost $51 and bed with breakfast and supper cost $57. On Saturdays and during the month of August, add $5 to these prices.

Space on tent platforms is $7 per night. Camping is not allowed in the vicinity of the huts and is problematic anyway. The rocky nature of the terrain makes tent camping difficult. The beauty of the huts is that with bed and meals (except lunch) provided, hikers can travel unencumbered by heavy packs.

Travel through the White Mountains, because of the high cost of the huts, is a challenge for thru-hikers. In the past, some thru-hikers have been allowed to stay at the huts in exchange for doing kitchen or other work. This benefit is not offered to all hikers and thru-hikers, and depends on the good will and generosity of the individual hut leaders. In other words, don't plan on it. The AMC Huts, except for Carter Hut and Zealand Hut with year-around caretakers, are closed during the winter. The others open in the first week of June and close in the middle of September. Information about the AMC Hut System may be accessed by calling (603) 466-2725. Reservations may be made by calling (603) 466-2727. Or write to the AMC Hut System, Box 298, Gorham, New Hampshire 03581. In any event, make contact well in advance of any planned visits because the huts fill quickly during the summer.

ROAN MOUNTAIN MASSIF

In the southern Appalachians, one of the most scenic sections of the AT is the 15 miles of the Roan Mountain Massif on the Tennessee/North Carolina Border. Roan High Nob, Round Bald, Jane Bald and Hump Mountain along with Grassy Ridge are some of the finest balds in the southern Appalachians and offer unparalleled panoramas. The vistas are inspiring at any time of the year, but in late June, when the rhododendrons and flame azaleas are in bloom, the mountains become a feast of color. Flaming orange, deep purple, lavender and pale yellow from the summer palette splash across the forest greens in great bursts of floral exuberance. Dotting the hillsides in July one can often find the reddish-orange Gray's Lilies, flowers unique to this region. Roan Mountain rises over 6,000 feet into the sky, and Round and Jane Balds are well over 5,000 feet. On clear days from Hump Mountain, one can see the Doe River Valley with Whitetop and Mount Rogers, two of the highest mountains in Virginia, framed by the blue-tinged horizon in the distance.

The Roan can be reached by following US 19E north out of Elk Park, North Carolina, into the northern section of the Massif. Tennessee Route 143 from Roan Mountain, Tennessee, and North Carolina Route 261 from Bakersville, North Carolina, both lead to Carvers Gap in the southern Roan. Even with nearby summits offering exceptional views, relatively few visitors leave the vicinity of Carvers Gap or the parking area on Roan High Nob. The result is that the more adventurous often find themselves sharing the vistas and the wilderness with only the wildlife.

GRAYSON HIGHLANDS and VICINITY

The section covering Mount Rogers, Whitetop Mountain and the Grayson Highlands of southern Virginia is probably the best kept secret of the Appalachian Trail. Because of its remoteness, it is visited by relatively few people, which makes it inviting to those seeking solitude.

Mount Rogers, the highest point in Virginia (5,729 ft.), is heavily forested with no views; however, Buzzards Rock on Whitetop Mountain and the Alpine meadows of Pine Mountain offer excellent views. Whitetop is a veritable wildflower garden in the spring, and Pine Mountain and Rhododendron Gap are covered by purple rhododendrons in June.

The Grayson Highlands contain a wide range of absolutely intriguing rock formations reminding visitors of scenery from western movies. One almost expects to see horses and riders racing over the horizon. In fact, there are many horse trails through the entire area, and hikers will almost certainly encounter members of small bands of wild horses grazing on the lush grass of the high meadows. Some of the horses have become accustomed to hikers and will actually approach you. Cattle also graze the range around the highlands.

The Grayson Highlands State Park Campground is just down the road a couple of miles from Massie Gap which is .5 miles from the AT on Wilburn Ridge. It offers campsites and has sanitary facilities including hot showers. Ideally located for day hiking through the area, the Campground is only 1.2 miles south of the Trail crossing of Wilson Creek.

The northern end of the section may be reached via Virginia Route 603 out of Konnarock, Virginia, and Virginia Route 16 out of Troutdale. US 58 leads to the southern end about 14 miles east of Damascus, Virginia. In the middle, Virginia Route 600 crosses the Trail at Elk Garden between Mount Rogers and Whitetop Mountain.

GREAT SMOKY MOUNTAINS

The Great Smoky Mountains National Park is a hugely popular vacation area during the summer; those desiring solitude will probably not find it there at that time. But its spectacular beauty and the views from various balds and summits more than make up for this shortcoming. The Trail winds for 70 miles through the Smokies and traverses the highest point on the AT at Clingmans Dome (6,643 ft.). The wildlife in the Park is not hunted and has lost its fear of humans. It is not unusual to approach within a few feet of browsing whitetail deer. In fact, if you are near any succulent looking plantain, the deer will probably approach you.

The Park's black bears are notorious for plundering unattended packs, and rangers admonish hikers to keep their packs secured at all times. Bears are quite numerous in the park and anyone hiking the AT or any of the other trails is sure to see one or two.

There are 800 miles of trails through the park; hikers have ample opportunity for exploration. Those desiring to hike the entire 70 miles of the AT in the Park usually start at Fontana Dam in the west/south or Davenport Gap and the Pigeon River in the east/north. There are no points to reprovision along the Trail; hikers must carry enough food to last the entire 70 mile journey.

Hikers planning to camp or stay at the Park's shelters must obtain permits from the National Park Service prior to entering the Park. This can be done at the Fontana Village Ranger Station, the Visitor's Center at Fontana Dam, the Big Creek Ranger Station near Davenport Gap or any other ranger station or visitor's center. Hikers can also get permits from the USFS French Broad Ranger District Headquarters in Hot Springs, North Carolina. For further information, contact the Great Smoky Mountains National Park, Gatlinburg, Tennessee 37738.

The shelters along the AT in the Smokies are nicely spaced

with no more than ten miles between them and most only five to seven miles apart.

Among the many places with spectacular scenery are Clingmans Dome with its observation tower. In clear weather, the tower offers great views for 360 degrees. From Charlies Bunion, a gigantic rock formation, there are views of Mount LeConte, Jump-Off, Mount Kephart, the gorges on the headwaters of Porters Creek and Greenbrier Pinnacle. Any number of the open summits such as Mounts Buckley or Thunderhead also offer magnificent views.

Davenport Gap may be reached by Interstate Route 40 between Knoxville, Tennessee, and Asheville, North Carolina, and US Route 70. Fontana Dam and Fontana Village can be reached by US Route 19 west of Bryson City, North Carolina, and North Carolina Route 28.

SHENANDOAH NATIONAL PARK

For those living in the coastal corridor between Baltimore, Maryland, and Richmond, Virginia, the Shenandoah National Park also provides a close-in opportunity for a wilderness experience. However, it, even more than the Great Smoky Mountains National Park, attracts visitors during the summer and in the fall when the leaves change color. Most people are attracted to the Park because of the ease of access. The Skyline Drive traverses the length of the Park and allows visitors to admire the scenery simply by stopping at various overlooks.

Still, the AT, which parallels the Skyline Drive, remains remarkably unspoiled. In those places removed from tourist attractions such as Big Meadows and Skyland, one can often find solitude and a pristine natural environment. In addition to the 103 miles of the AT, about 150 separate side trails of varying lengths and difficulty throughout the Park offer hikers escape from the crowds along Skyline Drive.

One unique aspect of Shenandoah National Park is its waterfalls. There are 16 of them, varying in heights from 22 feet at the Lower Rose River Falls to 93 feet at Big Falls on Overall Run.

The number of shelters, called huts in the Park, is more than adequate for basic hikers. For those interested in more luxurious accommodations, The Potomac Appalachian Trail Club also maintains six locked cabins that can be reserved through the Club. As in the Smokies, the National Park Service requires backpacker registration. Registration may be accomplished at Ranger checkpoints at either the northern entrance to the Park near Front Royal, Virginia, or the southern entrance at Rockfish Gap.

A wide range of wildlife, including nearly tame deer and less tame black bears, as well as the secretive bobcat, is at home in the Park. There are even reports of mountain lion sightings.

A number of major highways, US Routes 211, 33, 250 and I-64, cross the Blue Ridge, either adjacent to or through the Park making access easy.

MAINE

The AT in the entire state of Maine is relatively remote, and except for weekends and the more popular scenic attractions in the south like Mahoosuc Notch, hikers will pretty much have the Trail to themselves. If solitude and a magnificent natural environment are primary desires, then Maine is the place to hike. However, once on the Trail in Maine, it is difficult to resupply. This is especially true of the stretch between Monson and Baxter State Park. This 100 mile length of trail crosses a couple of well-maintained, unpaved logging roads, but that is about the only human intrusion into the wilderness.

Water is everywhere. Thousands of crystalline lakes, and clear rushing rivers and streams, along with a few roads and some spectacular mountain ridges such as Chairback, Saddleback, Moxie Bald and Bald Pate are all that break the seemingly unending undulations of forest in all directions.

For those with the time, Maine in the mid-to-late summer, after the black fly season, is a hiker's dream. The scenery is spectacular everywhere, and there are some 279 miles of AT to explore. Abundant wildlife, spruce grouse, loons, black bear, whitetail deer and, of course, moose inhabit the forests and lakes throughout the region. The people along the Trail in Maine can be compared to the pioneers. The frontier spirit is alive and well. Helping one's neighbor is a tradition. For those acculturated to the indifference and rudeness that sometimes passes for urban civilization, a visit to villages along the AT in Maine can be a refreshing experience.

The AT covers over 2,158 miles through 14 states. Each has splendid hiking areas with rewarding natural environments. Every hiker has their own favorite piece of the planet. Those mentioned here are the ones that most impressed me. I urge you to explore the AT on your own. There are many hidden treasures to be found and wonderful adventures to be enjoyed.

Happy Trails!

Appendix: ATC & Member Trail-Maintaining Clubs

The Trail-Maintaining Clubs are the lifeblood of the Appalachian Trail Conference. Their members are the people who clear and maintain the pathway, relocate the Trail, and when necessary build the bridges, privies and shelters, improve water sources, compile the guidebooks and assist in land acquisition.

All who hike the Appalachian Trail owe an immense debt of gratitude to these people who labor in anonymity and who are rewarded only by their love of the Trail, knowing they are a part of its culture and history. It is a story of devotion to an ideal.

The following list is provided by the Appalachian Trail Conference, and it is reprinted here with their permission. Check the ATC website for updates and terrain reports.

ATC Central Office

Central Office
Appalachian Trail Conference
799 Washington St.
Harpers Ferry, WV 25425
phone (304) 535-6331
email: info@atconf.org or info@appalachiantrail.org
http://www.atconf.org or http://www.appalachiantrail.org

ATC Regional Offices

New England Regional Office
Appalachian Trail Conference
P. O. Box 312
Lyme, NH 03768
Phone (603) 795-4936
Email: ATC-nero@atconf.org

Mid Atlantic Regional Office
Appalachian Trail Conference
P. O. Box 381
Boiling Springs, PA 17007
Phone (717) 258-5771
Email: ATC-maro@atconf.org

Central and Southwest
Virginia Office
Appalachian Trail Conference
P. O. Box 10
Newport, VA 24128
phone (540) 544-7388
Email: ATC-varo@atconf.org

Tennessee, North Carolina
and Georgia Office
Appalachian Trail Conference
P. O. Box 2750
Asheville, NC 28802
Phone (828) 254-3708
Email: ATC-gntro@atconf.org

Appalachian Trail Maintaining Clubs
(In order of Trail assignments—south to north)

Georgia Appalachian Trail club
P.O. Box 654
Atlanta, GA 30301
Phone (404) 634-6495
http://www.georgia-atclub.org
Springer Mountain, GA,
to Bly Gap, NC

Nantahala Hiking Club
Franklin, NC
http://www.smnet2.net/users/nhc
Bly Gap to Wesser, NC

Smoky Mountains Hiking Club
P.O. Box 1454
Knoxville, TN 37901
http://www.esper.com/smhc
Wesser, NC, to Davenport
Gap, TN/NC

Carolina Mountain Club
P.O. Box 68
Asheville, NC 28802
http://www.carolinamtnclub.com
Davenport Gap to
Spivey Gap, NC

Tennessee Eastman Hiking Club
P.O. Box 511
Kingsport, TN 37662
http://www.tehcc.org
Spivey Gap to Damascus, VA

Mt. Rogers Appalachian
Trail club
Damascus to VA 670

Note: Three existing clubs are maintaining the 20.2 miles between VA 615 north to VA 608; these temporary assignments are available for a new club (or clubs) to become involved in A.T. maintainance.

Piedmont Appalachian
Trail Hikers
P.O. Box 4423
Greensboro, NC 27404
http://www.path-at.org
VA 670 to VA 623;
VA 615 north to I-77 temporarily

Outdoor Club of Virginia Tech
P.O. Box 538
Blacksburg, VA 24060
http://www.fbox.vt.edu/org/outing/
VA 623 to VA 615;
I-77 to VA 611 temporarily
US 460 to Pine Swamp Shelter

Roanoke Appalachian Trail club
P.O. Box 12282
Roanoke, VA 24024
http://www.ratc.org
VA 608 to to Black Horse Gap.
VA 611 to VA 608 temporarily except US 460 to Pine Swamp Shelter.

Natural Bridge Appalachian
Trail club
P.O. Box 3012
Lynchburg, VA 24503
http://www.inmind.com/nbatc
Black Horse Gap to Tye River

Tidewater Appalachian
Trail club
P.O. Box 8246
Norfolk, VA 23503
http://www.geocities.com/Yosemite/
Tye River to Reeds Gap

Old Dominion Appalachian
Trail club
P.O. Box 25283
Richmond, VA 23260
http://www.ODATC.org
Reeds Gap to Rockfish Gap

Potomac Appalachian
Trail club
Vienna, VA
Phone: (703) 242-0693
http://www.patc.net
Rockfish Gap, VA, to Pine Grove
Furnace State Park, PA

Potomac Appalachian
Trail club (PATC)
Local Chapters
*(visit the ATC or PATC website
for up-to-date contact information)*

•Charlottesville Chapter
•Southern Shenandoah Valley
Chapter
•Northern Shenandoah Valley
Chapter
•West Virginia Chapter
•North Chapter
•Mountain Club of Maryland

http://www.mcomd.org

Pine Grove Furnace State Park,
PA, to Center Point Knob and
Darlington Trail to Susquehanna
River

Cumberland Valley
Appalachian Trail club
P.O. Box 395
Boiling Springs, PA 17007
http://www.community.
pennlive.com/cc/
Center Point Knob to
Darlington Trail

York Hiking Club
York, PA
http://www.angelfire.com/pa2/
yorkhikingclub/index.html
Susquehanna River to PA 225

Susquehanna Appalachian
Trail club
Box 610001
Harrisburg, PA 17106-1001
www.libertynet.org/susqatc
PA 225 to Clarks Valley

Brandywine Valley Outing Club
P.O. Box 134
Rockland, DE 19732
Clarks Valley to Rausch Creek

Blue Mountain Eagle Climbing
Club
P.O. Box 14982
Reading, PA 19612-4982
http://www.bmecc.org
Rausch Creek to Tri-County Cor-
ner and Bake Oven Knob to
Lehigh Furnace Gap

Allentown Hiking Club
P.O. Box 1542
Allentown, PA 18105-1542
http://www.allentownhikingclub.org
Tri-County Corner to Bake Oven Knob

Philadelphia Trail club
Warrington, PA
Lehigh Furnace Gap to Little Gap

AMC-Delaware Valley Chapter
Bethlehem, PA
http://www.amcdv.org
Little Gap to Wind Gap

Batona Hiking Club
Philadelphia, PA
http://www.members.aol.com/Batona
Wind Gap to Fox Gap

Wilmington Trail club
P.O. Box 1184
Wilmington, DE 19899
http://www.wilmingtontrailclub.org
Fox Gap to Delaware River, PA

New York-New Jersey Trail Conference
Mahwah, NJ
http://www.nynjtc.org
Delaware River, NJ, to CN/NY border

AMC-Connecticut Chapter
P.O. Box 1800
Lanesboro, MA 01237
http://www.ct-amc.org
CN/NY border to Sages Ravine

AMC-Berkshire Chapter
P.O. Box 1800
Lanesboro, MA 01237
http://www.amcberkshire.org
Sages Ravine (CN/MA) to VT/MA border

Green Mountain Club
Waterbury Center, VT
http://www.greenmountainclub.org
VT/MA border to VT 12

Dartmouth Outing Club
P.O. Box 9
Hanover, NH 03755
http://www.dartmouth.edu/~doc
VT 12 to Kinsman Notch, NH

Appalachian Mountain Club
P. O. Box 298
Gorham, NH 03581-0298
http://www.outdoors.org
Kinsman Notch, NH, to Grafton Notch, ME

Maine Appalachian Trail club
P.O. Box 283
Augusta, ME 04332-0283
http://www.matc.org
Grafton Notch to Katahdin

OF RELATED INTEREST

Appalachian Long Distance
Hikers Association
West Lebanon, NH
http://www.aldha.org
Organizes work trips on the AT

A.T. Home Page
http://www.fred.net/kathy/html

Appalachian Trailplace
http://www.trailplace.com

Keystone Trails Association
Box 251
Cogan Station, PA 17728
http://www.pennaweb.com/kt
KTA is the umbrella organization for clubs throughout PA,
some of which maintain the AT

Appalachian National
Scenic Trail
http://www.nps.gov/appa/

A.T. Club of Florida
Email: gatyner@ix.netcom.com
ATC Supporting Organization

A.T. Club of Alabama
P.O. Box 381842
Birmingham, Alabama 35238
http://www.sport.al.com/sport/
atca

Lower Appalachian Trail Assoc.
507 Broadway
Sylacauga, AL 35150

Illinois A.T. Club
Email: nsimon@megsinet.net

International Appalachian Trail
Freeport, Maine
http://www.internationalat.org

Appendix: Post Offices Within Six Miles of the AT

Hours of Post Office operation differ from town to town and sometimes change with the season. For that reason, telephone numbers are included to aid in planning or for coordinating with local Postal personnel. Often times, a call ahead may help get a back door to the Post Office opened at other than normal operating hours. My experience has been that the Postal people are very sympathetic toward thru-hikers and often go out of their way to help.

Post Office	Distance From the AT	Telephone Number
Suches, GA 30572	1.6 miles west	(706) 747-2611
Fontana Dam, NC 28733	2 miles west	(704) 498-2315
Hot Springs, NC 28743	On the AT	(704) 622-3242
Erwin, TN 37650	3.8 miles west	(615) 743-4811
Elk Park, NC 28622	2.5 miles east	(704) 733-5711
Hampton, TN 37658	2.6 miles west	(615) 725-3703
Damascus, VA 24236	On the AT	(703) 475-3411
Troutdale, VA 24378	2.6 miles east	(703) 677-3221
Atkins, VA 24311	3.2 miles west	(703) 783-5551
Bastain, VA 24314	1.8 miles west	(703) 688-4631
Bland, VA 24315	2.5 miles east	(703) 688 3751
Pearisburg, VA 24134	1 mile east	(703) 921-1100

Catawba, VA 24070	1 mile west	(703) 384-6011
Cloverdale, VA 24077	1.2 miles west	(703) 992-2334
Troutville, VA 24175	.8 miles west	(703) 992-1472
Big Island, VA 24526	4.6 miles east	(804) 299-5072
Montebello, VA 24464	1.9 miles west	(703) 377-9218
Tyro, VA 22976	1.4 miles east	(804) 277-9401
Waynesboro, VA 22980	4.5 miles west	(703) 949-8129
Front Royal, VA 22630	4.2 miles west	(703) 635-4540
Linden, VA 22642	1 mile west	(703) 636-9936
Harpers Ferry, WV 25425	.5 miles west	(304) 535-2479
Burkittsville, MD 21718	1.2 miles east	(301) 834-9944
Boonesboro, MD 21713	2.4 miles west	(301) 432-6861
Blue Ridge Summit, PA 17214	2.2 miles east	(717) 794-2335
South Mountain, PA 17261	1.2 miles east	(717) 749-5833
Boiling Springs, PA 17007	On the AT	(717) 258-6668
Duncannon, PA 17020	On the AT	(717) 834-3332
Pine Grove, PA 17963	3.7 miles west	(717) 345-4955
Port Clinton, PA 19549	On the AT	(610) 562-3787
Palmerton, PA 18071	2 miles west	(610) 826-2286
Wind Gap, PA 18091	1 mile east	(610) 863-6106
Delaware Water Gap, PA 18327	.1 miles west	(717) 476-0304
Branchville, NJ 07826	3.4 miles east	(201) 948-3580
Unionville, NY 10988	.4 miles west	(914) 726-3535
Vernon, NJ 07462	2.4 miles east	(201) 764-2920
Arden, NY 10910	.7 miles west	(914) 351-5341
Fort Montgomery, NY 10922	.7 miles west	(914) 446-2173
Stormville, NY 12582	1.9 miles west	(914) 221-9710
Pawling, NY 12564	2.9 miles east	(914) 855-1010
Kent, CT 06757	.8 miles east	(203) 927-3435
Cornwall Bridge, CT 06754	.9 miles east	(203) 672-6710
Falls Village, CT 06031	.5 miles east	(203) 824-7781
Salisbury, CT 06068	.8 miles west	(203) 435-9485
South Egremont, MA 01258	1.2 miles west	(413) 528-1571
Tyringham, MA 011264	.9 miles west	(413) 243-0419
Dalton, MA 01226	.3 miles east	(413) 684-0364
Cheshire, MA 10225	On the AT	(413) 743-3184
North Adams, MA 01247	2.5 miles east	(413) 664-4554
Bennington, VT 05201	5.1 miles west	(802) 442-2421

Manchester Center, VT 05255	5.5 miles east	(802) 362-3070
Killington, VT 05751	3.6 miles east	(802) 775-4247
South Pomfret, VT 05067	.9 miles east	(802) 457-1147
West Hartford, VT 05084	.2 miles east	(802) 295-6239
Norwich, VT 05055	.5 miles west	(802) 649-1608
Hanover, NH 03755	On the AT	(603) 643-4544
Lyme Center, NH 03769	1.2 miles west	(603) 989-5858
Glencliff, NH 03238	.5 miles east	(603) 795-2688
North Woodstock, NH 03262	5.8 miles east	(603) 745-8134
Mt. Washington, NH 03589*	On the AT	(603) 846-5404
Gorham, NH 03581	3.6 miles west	(603) 466-2182
Andover , ME 04216**	8 miles east	(207) 392-4571
Rangeley, ME 04970 **	9 miles west	(207) 864-2233
Stratton, ME 04982	5 miles west	(207) 246-6461
Caratunk, ME 04925	.3 miles east	(207) 672-5532
Monson, ME 04464	2 miles east	(207) 997-3975

* Mt. Washington is often closed during periods of severe weather. It is not advisable to use this Post Office for mail drops.

** Towns in Maine **not** within six miles of the Trail, but these Post Offices are all that is available for mail drops. Therefore, they have been included.

Note: Do not send UPS or Federal Express parcels to Post Offices. Such parcels will not be accepted or held by the US Postal Service.

Appendix: Bibliography

Ambling and Scrambling on the Appalachian Trail, James M. & Hertha E. Flack, 1981, The Appalachian Trail Conference.

The Appalachian Scenic Trail, A Time to be Bold, Charles H.W. Foster, 1987.

The Appalachian Trail: A Journey of Discovery, Jan D. Curran, Rainbow Books, Highland City, FL, 1991.

The Appalachian Trail Backpacker, Victoria and Frank Logue, Menasha Ridge Press, Birmingham, AL, 1991.

The Appalachian Trail Conference Backpacker's Recipe Book, Steve Antell, Pruett Publishing Company, Boulder CO, 1980.

Appalachian Trail Conference Member Handbook, Appalachian Trail Conference, Inc.,1988.

Appalachian Trail Data Book, Edited by Daniel D. Chazin and revised yearly.

The Audubon Society Field Guide to North American Mammals, Alfred A. Knopf, Inc., 1980.

The Audubon Society Field Guide to North American Trees, Eastern Region, Alfred A. Knopf, Inc., 1980.

The Audubon Society Field Guide to North American Wildflowers, Alfred A. Knopf, Inc., 1979.

Backpacker, The Magazine of Wilderness Travel, Rodale Press, Inc., Emmaus, PA, Published nine times per year.

Backwoods Ethics, 2nd Edition, Laura and Guy Waterman, The Countryman Press, Woodstock, VT, 1993.

The Complete Walker III, 3rd Edition, Colin Fletcher, Alfred A. Knopf, NY, 1993.

Comprehensive Plan for the Protection, Management, Development and Use of the Appalachian National Scenic Trail, The Appalachian Trail Project Office, National Park Service, Harpers Ferry, WVA, September 1981.

The Earth-Man Story, Parks, Man, and his Environment, Darwin Lambert, 1972, Exposition Press, Inc.

A Field Guide to the Birds, East of the Rockies, Roger Tory Peterson, Houghton Mifflin Company, Boston, 1980.

Gorp, Glop & Glue Stew Favorite Foods from 165 Outdoor Experts, Yvonne Prater and Ruth Dyar Mendenhall, The Mountaineers, Seattle, WA, 1981.

The Healthy Trail Food Book, Dorcas S. Miller, The East Woods Press, 1976.

Master Tree Finder, A Manual for the Identification of Trees by their Leaves, May Theilgaard Watts, Nature Study Guild, 1963.

Mountain Adventure, Exploring the Appalachian Trail, Ron Fisher, Photographs by Sam Abell, National Geographic Society, 1988.

Mountaineering Medicine, A Wilderness Medical Guide, Fred T. Darvill, Jr., M.D., Wilderness Press, Berkeley, CA, 1992.

The New Exploration, A Philosophy of Regional Planning, Benton MacKaye, Harcourt, Brace & Co, Inc., 1928, Benton MacKaye, 1956, Board of Trustees of the University of Illinois, 1962, Christy MacKaye Barnes, 1990.

The 1986 and 1987 Philosopher's Guides: Tips for AT Thru-Hikers, Darrell Maret, The Appalachian Trail Conference, 1986 — 1987.

The Thru-Hiker's Handbook: #1 Guide for Long-Distance Hikes on the Appalachian Trail . . . with town maps and mileage data from Georgia to Maine, Dan "Wingfoot" Bruce, Center for Appalachian Studies, 1995.

The Thru-Hiker's Planning Guide, Dan "Wingfoot" Bruce, Center for Appalachian Trail Studies, 1994.

Two On the Trail — Thousand Miles on the PCT — Pacific Crest Trail, Ann Marshall, 1985, Washington Trails Association.

Underfoot — A Geologic Guide to the Appalachian Trail, 2nd Edition, V. Collins Chew, Appalachian Trail Conference, Harpers Ferry, WVA, 1988.

Walden or Life in the Woods and On the Duty of Civil Disobedience, Henry David Thoreau, New American Library, Afterword, 1960, Bibliography 1980, both by New American Library, Signet Classic.

Walking With Spring, The First Thru-Hike of the Appalachian Trail, Earl V. Shaffer, 1983, The Appalachian Trail Conference.

Wilderness Visionaries, Marshall, Muir, Olson, Rutstrum, Service, Thoreau, Jim Dale Vickery, ICS Books, Inc., 1986.

The eleven official *Appalachian Trail Guides* with Maps: Maine, New Hampshire/Vermont, Massachusetts/Connecticut, New York/

New Jersey, Pennsylvania, Maryland/Northern Virginia, Shenandoah National Park, Central Virginia, Southwest Virginia, Tennessee/North Carolina, North Carolina/Georgia.

Appendix: Equipment Manufacturers

Listed below are the names, addresses, telephone numbers and websites of some hiking equipment manufacturers. Listing is by equipment type so duplication may occur in cases where firms manufacture more than one type of equipment. For brevity, only larger manufacturers are listed. More complete listings, along with testers' comments, can be found in *Backpacker* magazine, particularly the annual equipment review issue.

PACKS

Camp Trails
625 Conklin Rd.
Binghamton, NY 13903
phone (800) 345-7622
http://www.camptrails.com

Cascade Designs
4000 First Ave., S.
Seattle, WA 98134
phone (800) 531-9531
http://www.cascadedesigns.com

Coleman Exponent
3600 N. Hydraulic
Wichita, KS 67219
phone (800) 835-3278
http://www.coleman.com

Dana Design
19215 Vashon Hwy, SW
Vashon, WA 98070
phone (888) 357-3262
http://www.danadesign.com

PACKS, *continued*

Jack Wolfskin
1766A Fesler St.
El Cajon, CA 92020
phone (888) 378-9653

JanSport, Inc.
850 County Hwy., C.B.
Appleton, WI
phone (920) 831-2288
http://www.jansport.com

Kelty Pack, Inc.
6225 Lookout Rd.
Boulder, CO 80301
phone (800) 423-2320
http://www.kelty.com

L.L.Bean, Inc.
Casco St.
Freeport, ME 04033
phone (800) 809-7057
http://www.llbean.com

Lowe Alpine System
2325 W. Midway Blvd.
Broomfield, CO 80028
phone (303) 465-3706
http://www.lowealpine.com

Mountainsmith, Inc.
18301 W. Colfax Ave.
Building P
Golden, CO 80401
phone (303) 279-5930
http://www.mountainsmith.com

The North Face
2013 Farallon Dr.
San Leandro, CA 94577
phone (800) 535-3331
http://www.thenorthface.com

REI/Recreational Equipment
6750 S. 228 St.
Kent, WA 98032
phone (800) 426-4840
http://www.rei.com

TENTS

Bibler Tents
2084 E. 3900 South
Salt Lake City, UT 84124
phone (801) 278-5533
http://www.biblertents.com

Eastern Mountain Sports
One Vose Farm Road
Peterborough, NH 03458
phone (603) 924-9571
http://www.emsonline.com

TENTS, *continued*

Eureka!
1326 Willow Rd.
Sturtevant, WI 53117
phone (800) 345-7622
http://www.eurekatent.com

Integral Designs, Inc.
5516 Third St. S.E.
Calgary, Alberta
Canada T2H 1J9
phone (403) 640-1445
http://www.integraldesigns.com

Kelty, Inc.
6035 Lookout Rd.
Boulder, CO 80301
phone (800) 423-2320
http://www.kelty.com

Moss Tents
3800 First St., S.
Seattle, WA 98134
phone (800) 877-9677
http://www.mosstents.com

Mountain Hardwear
4911 Central Ave.
Richmond, CA 98408
phone (800) 953-8375
http://www.mountainhardware.com

Noall Tents
59530 Devils Ladder Rd.
26 Garner Valley
Mountain Center, CA 92561
phone (909) 659-4219

The North Face
2013 Farallon Dr.
San Leandro, CA 94577
phone (800) 535-3331
http://www.thenorthface.com

REI/Recreational Equipment
6750 S. 228 St.
Kent, WA 98032
phone (800) 426-4840
http://www.rei.com

Sierra Designs
1355 Powell St.
Emeryville, CA 94608
phone (800) 635-0461
http://www.sierradesigns.com

Walrus, Inc.
3800 First Ave., S.
Seattle, WA 98124
phone (800) 877-9677
http://www.walrusgear.com

BOOTS

Hundreds of firms manufacture boots. This listing includes only some of the major manufacturers.

Adidas, USA, Inc.
9605 SW Nimbus Ave.
Beaverton, OR 97008
phone (800) 677-6638
http://www.adidas.com

Alpina Sports Corp.
P.O. Box 23
Etna Rd.
Hanover, NH 03755
phone (603) 448-3101
http://www.alpinasports.com

Asolo USA Inc.
190 Hannover St.
Lebanon, NH 05766
phone (603) 448-8827
http://www.alsolo.com

Danner Shoe Mfg. Co.
12722 N.E. Airport Way
Portland, OR 97230
phone (800) 345-0430
http://www.danner.com

Eastern Mountain Sports
1 Vose Farm Road
Peterborough, NH 03458
phone (603) 924-9591
http://www.emsonline.com

Five Ten Co.
1419 W. State St.
P. O. Box 1185
Redlands, CA 92373
phone (909) 798-4222
http://www.fiveten.com

Garmont USA
170 Boyer Circle
Ste. 20
Williston, VT 05495
phone (802) 658-8322
http://www.garmontusa.com

Hi-Tec Sports USA, Inc.
4801 Stoddard Rd.
Modesto, CA 95356
phone (209) 545-1111
http://www.hitec.com

LA Sportiva USA
3280 Pearl St.
Boulder, CO 80403
phone (303) 443-8710
http://www.lasportiva.com

Lowa Boot, LLC
P. O. Box 407
Greenwich, CT 06870
phone (203) 353-0116
http://www.lowaboots.com

BOOTS, *continued*

Merrell Performance Footwear
9341 Courtland Dr.
Rockford, MI 49351
phone (888) 637-7001

Montrail, Inc.
1003 Sixth Ave., S.
Seattle, WA 98134
phone (800) 647-0224
http://www.montrail.com

Nike ACG
One Bowerman Dr.
Beaverton, OR 97005
http://www.nike.com

Raichle Outdoor
P. O. Box 2913
1240 Huff Lane
Jackson, WY 83001
phone (307) 733-2266
http://www.raichleoutdoor.com

Salomon North America
9401 SW Nimbus Ave.
Beaverton, OR 97008
phone (877) 272-5666
http://www.saloman-sports.com

Tecnica USA
19 Technology Dr.
West Lebanon, NH 03784
phone (603) 298-8032
http://www.tecnicausa.com

Vasque
314 Main St.
Red Wing, MN 55066
phone (800) 224-4453
http://www.vasque.com

Wolverine Boots & Shoes
9341 Courtland Dr., NE
Rockford, MI 49351
phone (888) 927-9675
(http://)
www.wolverinebootsandshoes.com

SLEEPING BAGS

Alps Mountaineering
1 White Pine
New Haven, MO 63068
phone (573) 459-2577
(http://)
www.alpsmountaineering.com

Coleman Exponent
3600 N. Hydraulic
Wichita, KS 67219
phone (800) 835-3278
http://www.coleman.com

SLEEPING BAGS, *continued*

Eastern Mountain Sports
One Vose Farm Road
Peterborough, NH 03458
phone (603) 924-9571
http://www.emsonline.com

Feathered Friends
119 Yale Ave., N.
Seattle, WA 98109
phone (206) 292-6292
http://www.featheredfriends.com

Integral Designs
5516 Third St. SE
Calgary, Alberta
Canada T2H 1J9
phone (403) 640-1445
http://www.integraldesigns.com

Kelty, Inc.
6235 Lookout Rd.
Boulder, CO 80301
phone (800) 423-2320
http://www.kelty.com

L.L.Bean, Inc.
Casco St.
Freeport, ME 04033
phone (800) 809-7057
http://www.llbean.com

Marmot Mountain LTD
2321 Circadian Way
Santa Rosa, CA 95407
(707) 544-4590
http://www.marmot.com

Mountain Hardwear
494 Central Ave.
Richmond, CA 94808
phone (800) 953-8375
http://www.mountainhardwear.com

The North Face
2013 Farallon Dr.
San Leandro, CA 94577
phone (800) 535-3331
http://www.thenorthface.com

REI/Recreational Equipment
6750 S. 228 St.
Kent, WA 98032
phone (800) 426-4840
http://www.rei.com

Sierra Designs
1355 Powell St.
Emeryville, CA 94608
phone (800) 635-0461
http://www.sierradesigns.com

Slumberjack
1224 Fern Ridge Pkwy.
St. Louis, MO 63141
phone (800) 233-6283
http://www.slumberjack.com

Jack Wolfskin
1166-A Fesler St.
El Cajon, CA 92020
phone (888) 378-9653
http://www.wolfskin.com

SLEEPING PADS

Alpina Sports Corp.
P.O. Box 23
Etna Rd.
Hanover, NH 03755
phone (603) 448-3101
http://www.alpinasports.com

Appalachian Mountain Supply/
Artiach
731 Highland Ave.
Ste. C
Atlanta, GA 30312
phone (800) 569-4110
http://www.amsgear.com

Avid Outdoor
1120 W. 149 St.
Olathe, KS 66061
phone (913) 780-2843
http://www.avidoutdoor.com

Cascade Designs
4000 First Ave., S.
Seattle, WA 98134
phone (800) 531-9531
http://www.cascadedesigns.com

Crazy Creek Products, Inc.
1401 S. Broadway
P. O. Box 1050
Red Lodge, MT 59068
phone (800) 331-0304
http://www.crazycreek.com

High Country Outdoor Products
19767 SE Sunnyside Rd.
Damascus, OR 97009
phone (503) 658-4704
http://www.highcop.com

Mountain Hardwear
4911 Central Ave.
Richmond, CA 94804
phone (800) 953-8375
http://www.mountainhardwear.com

Slumberjack
1224 Fern Ridge Pkwy.
St. Louis, MO 63141
phone (800) 233-6283
http://www.slumberjack.com

Sterns, Inc.
P. O. Box 1498
St. Cloud, MN 56302
phone (320) 252-1642
http://www.sternsinc.com

SunnyRec Corp.
20505 Belshaw Ave.
Carson, CA 90746
phone (310) 638-4368
http://www.sunnyreccorp.com

STOVES

Coleman Exponent
3600 N. Hydraulic
Wichita, KS 67219
phone (800) 835-3278
http://www.coleman.com

MSR/Mountain Safety Research
3300 First Ave., S.
Seattle, WA 98134
phone (800) 877-9677
http://www.msrcorp.com

Optimus
620 E. Monroe Ave.
Riverton, WY 82501
phone (307) 856-6559
http://www.optimausa.com

Primus/Suunto USA
2151 Las Palmas Dr.
Ste. F
Carlsbad, CA 92009
phone (760) 931-6788
http://www.suuntousa.com

VauDe Sports, Inc.
P. O. Box 3413 Tavern Rd.
Mammoth Lakes, CA 93546
phone (800) 447-1539
http://www.vaude.com

ZZ Manufacturing
1520-A Industrial Park St.
Covina, CA 90722
phone (800) 594-9046
http://www.gorp.com/zzstove

WATER FILTERS

Exstream Water
Technologies, Inc.
1035 W. Bruce St.
Milwaukee, WI 53204
phone (800) 563-6968
http://www.exstreamwater.com

General Ecology, Inc.
151 Sheree Blvd.
Exton, PA 19341
phone (800) 441-8166
http://www.generalecology.com

Katadyn Suunto USA
2151 Las Palmas Dr.
Ste. F
Carlsbad, CA 92009
phone (800) 543-9124
http://www.suuntousa.com

MSR/Mountain Safety Research
3800 First Ave., S.
Seattle, WA 98134
phone (800) 877-9677
http://www.msrcorp.com

WATER FILTERS, *continued*

PUR
9300 N. 75th Ave.
Minneapolis, MN 55428
phone (800) 787-5463
http://www.purwater.com

SafeWater Anywhere
208 Oak St.
Ste. 106
Ashland, OR 97520
phone (800) 675-4401
http://www.safewateranywhere.com

WPC Brands, Inc.
1 Repel Rd.
P. O. Box 198
Jackson, WI 53037
phone (800) 558-6614
http://www.wpcbrands.com

CAMPING STORES ALONG THE TRAIL

These retailers are specific for camping equipment. You may also want to search a local or internet phone directory (preferably before you go) for sporting goods stores, general stores, and superstores like K-Mart and Wal-Mart.

BMO
(on the AT)
152 Bridge Street
Hot Springs, NC 28743
phone (828) 622-9626

Rockfish Gap Outfitters
(4.5 miles west of the AT)
1461 E. Main St.
Waynesboro, VA 22980
phone (540) 943-1461

Pack Shack Adventures, Inc.
(.1 mile west of the AT)
Broad
Delaware Water Gap, PA 18327
phone (570) 424-8533

Backcountry Outfitters
(.8 miles east of the AT)
Kent Green
Kent, CT 06757
phone (860) 927-3377

Dartmouth CO Op
(on the AT)
25 S. Main St.
Hanover, NH 03755
phone (603) 643-7252

INTERNET SITES FEATURING CAMPING/HIKING GEAR

123 Camping.com (http://www.123-camping.com/)
A1Camping.com (http://www.a1camping.com/)
Allen Outdoors Products (http://www.allenoutdoor.com/)
American Wilderness, Inc. (http://www.awigear.com/)
Appalachian Mountain Gear (http://www.amggear.com/)
Appalachian Mountain Supply (http://www.amsgear.com/)
Armitage Hardware (http://www.colemanoutdoors.com/)
Backcountry Gear Limited (http://www.backcountrygear.com/)
Backcountry Store (http://www.bcstore.com/)
Beaver Tree Camp Kitchens (http://www.beavertree.com/)
Blue Sky Kitchen (http://www.blueskykitchen.com/)
The Camping Source (http://www.thecampingsource.com/)
Campmor (http://www.campmor.com)
eBay Auctions (http://www.ebay.com/) check under "Sporting Goods"
Eureka Camping Center (http://www.eurekacampingctr.com/)
GearFind (http://www.gearfinder.com/)
Gorp.com (http://www.gorp.com)
A Happy Camper (http://www.ahappycamper.com/)
JMS Tooling (http://www.jms-tooling.com/)
Kirkhams Outdoor Products (http://www.kirkhams.com/)
Kondos Outdoors (http://www.kondosoutdoors.com/)
Montane (http://www.montane.com/)
Moosineer (http://www.moosineer.com/)
Mountain Zone (http://www.mountainzone.com/)
Myles Recreational Accessories (http://www.myles-rec.com/)
Norquest Innovation Corp. (http://www.polardome.com/)
Northward Bound (http://www.northwardbound.com/)
Outdoor Experience (http://www.gearpro.com/)
Outdoor Gear Exchange (http://www.gearx.com/)
Outdoor World (http://www.theoutdoorworld.com/)
Snow Leopard Mountain Sports (http://www.thesnowleopard.com/)
U.S. Navy SEAL Supply Store (http://www.thesealstore.com/)
Venture Outdoors (http://www.venture-outdoors.com/)
Yahoo Listings (http://dir.yahoo.com/Recreation/Outdoors/)

Appendix: Maps of the Appalachian Trail

Maps, as a rule, are a necessity in most wilderness situations, but the AT is so well marked that one can easily navigate without them. However, having topographic maps of the AT provides several advantages for a hiker: Maps allow one to prepare for changes in terrain; to plan distances; to orient oneself in relation to observable terrain features; to keep surprise to a minimum and to anticipate changes in Trail direction or the location of points of interest (shelters, road crossings, springs, historical sites). Also, the maps which accompany guide books contain Trail profiles which are valuable guides to the difficulty of the terrain.

The maps that follow provide an excellent guide for pinpointing major points of interest and towns along the AT. They are also very helpful in locating approaches to the Trail, which may be difficult to ascertain from the Trail Guide maps. These also allow readers to visually follow certain terrain features or prospective hikes described in the narrative portion of this book.

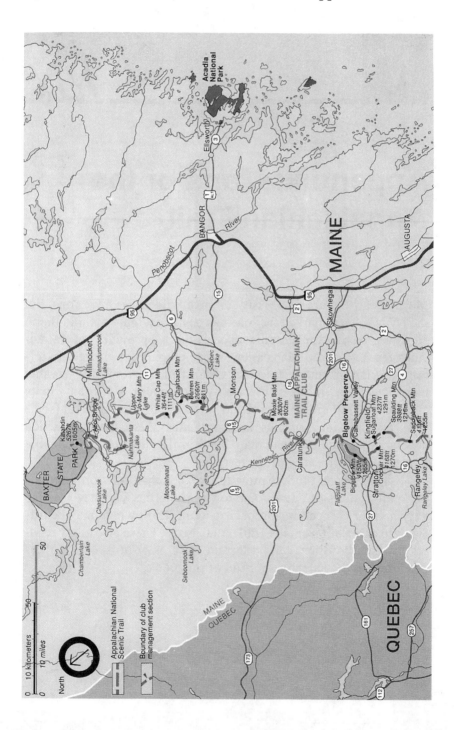

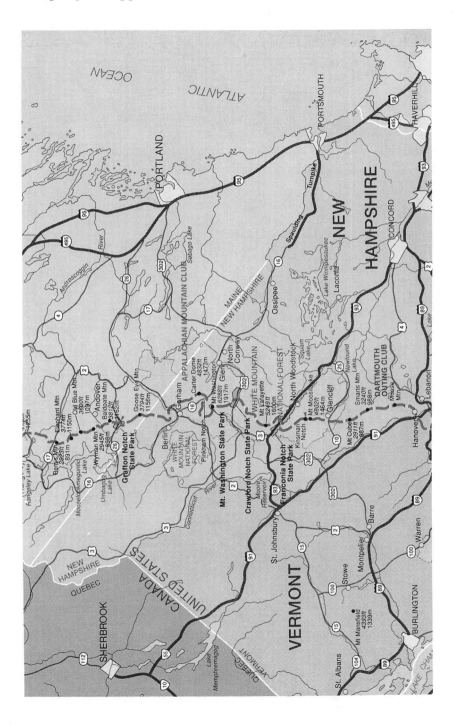

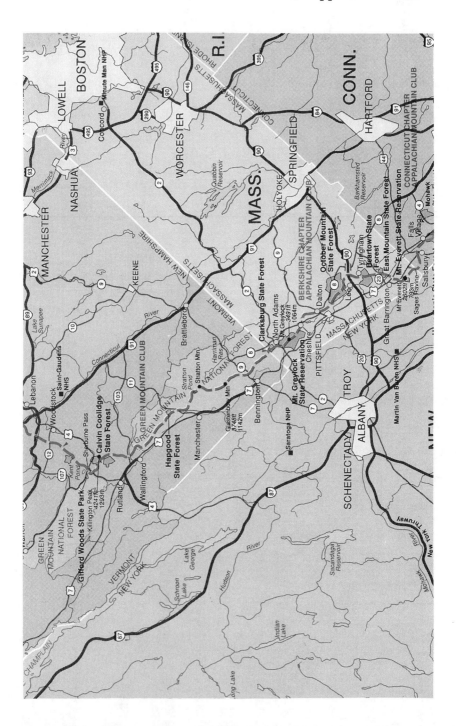

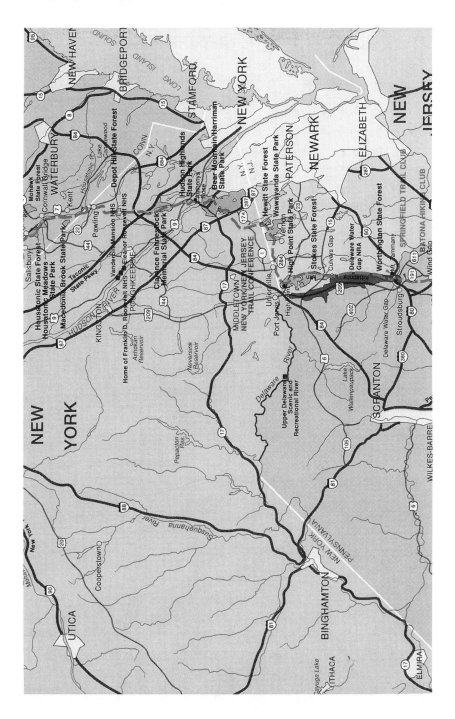

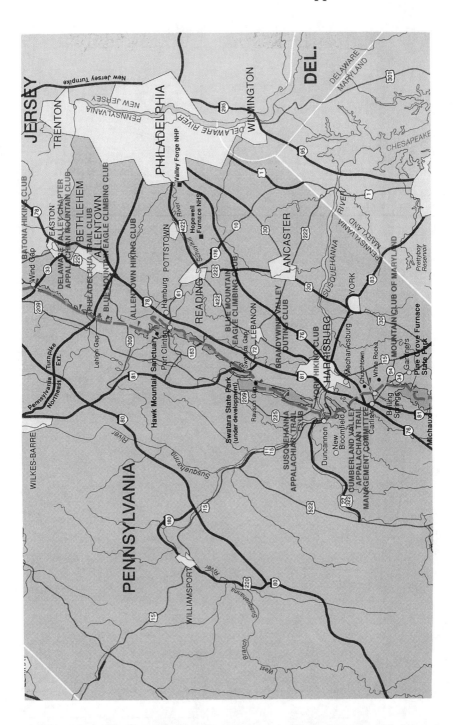

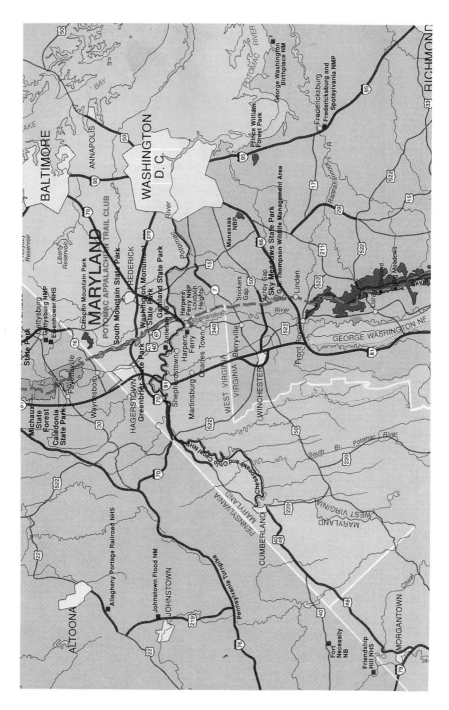

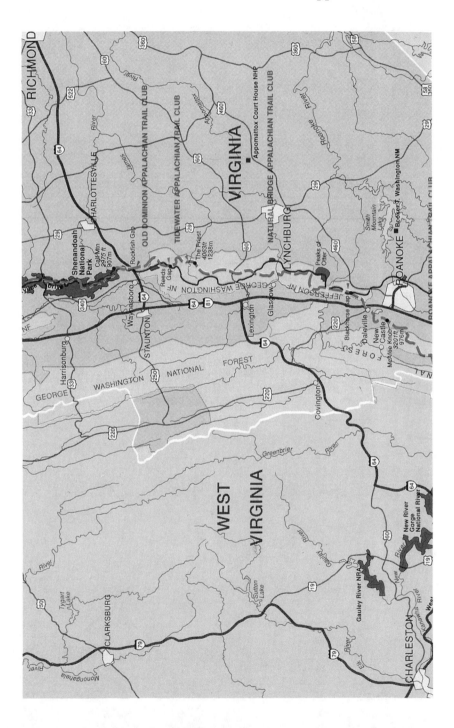

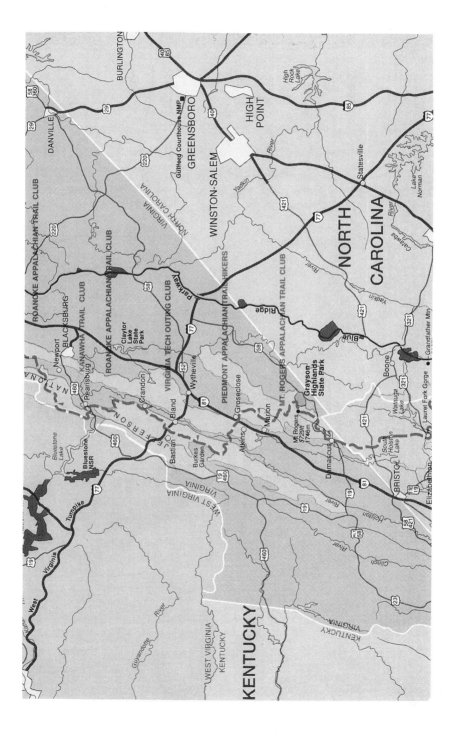

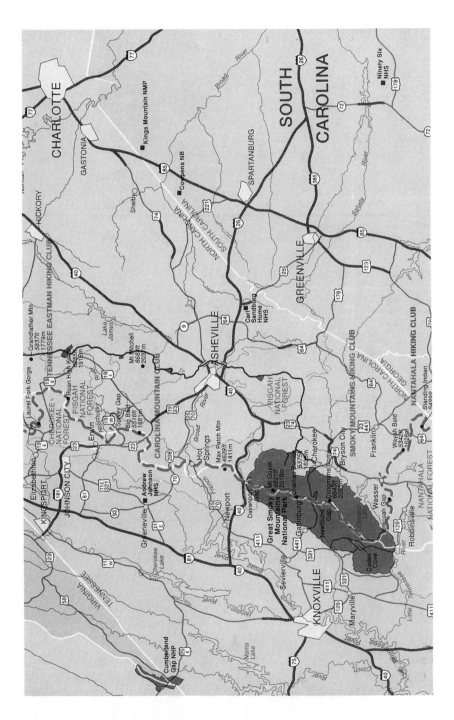

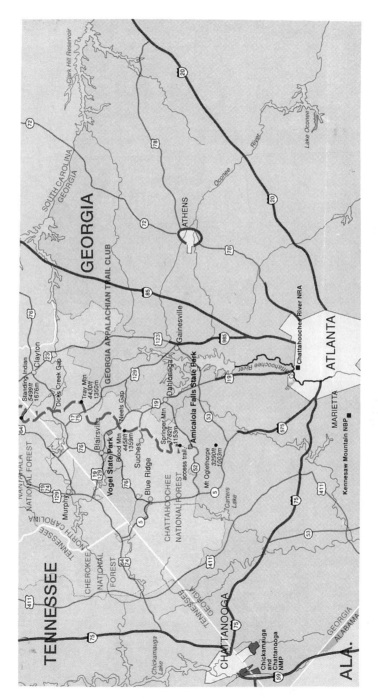

Reprinted with the permission of the National Park Service/U.S. Department of the Interior and the Appalachian Trail Conference.

Index

Symbols

123 Camping.com / 160
3M / 52
50th AT Anniversary Commemorative Hike / 61

A

A1Camping.com / 160
A.T. Club
    of Alabama / 142
    of Florida / 142
Abell, Sam / 148
Abenaki Indians / 21
Abol Campground, ME / 121, 127, *162*
Adidas (boots, shoes) / 40, 154
Adventure Medical Kits (first aid kits) / 78
Albany International Corp. (insulation) / 52
Albert Mountain, NC / 23, *170*
alcohol / 60, 73-74, 121-22
Allen Outdoors Products (website) / 160
Allentown Hiking Club / 140, *166*
Alpina Sports Corp. (boots, sleeping pads) / 154, 157
Alpine vegetation / 12, 31, 66, 119, 152
Alps Mountaineering (sleeping bags) / 155
AMC (Appalachian Mountain Club) / 15, 18, 141
    Berkshire Chapter of / 141, *164*
    Connecticut Chapter of / 141, *164*
    Delaware Valley Chapter of / 140, *166*
American Alpine Institute / 31

American Wilderness, Inc. (website) / 160
AMK (Adventure Medical Kits) / 79
Andover, ME / 145, *163*
animals / 58, 74, 81, 87, 89-104
    bats / 74, 96
    bears / 35, 62, 65, 89-90, 93-94, 97-98, 100, 118
    birds / 89, 95-98, 101, 103-104
    boars / 97, 98 (see also *hogs* and *pigs*)
    bobcats / 96-97
    coydogs / 95
    coyotes / 95-96
    deer / 26, 89-90, 95, 97-100, 106-107, 110
    dogs / 67, 72, 74-75, 95, 98, 106, 120
    eagles / 89
    elk / 100
    farm / 87
    foxes / 74, 95-96, 101
    frogs / 92, 97-98, 102
    grouse / 90-91, 97, 103
    hare / 96, 100-101 (see also *rabbits*)
    hawks / 89
    hogs / 22 (see also *boars* and *pigs*)
    lizards / 92
    mammals / 89, 102
    mice / 55, 65, 89-90, 96, 98, 128
    moose / 99-100
    opossum / 102
    pigmy rattlesnakes / 91
    pigs / 81, 97 (see also *boars* and *hogs*)
    pit vipers / 73, 92
    poisonous / 72, 91-92
    porcupines / 94, 96, 98-99
    predators / 89-90, 96-97, 102-103
    rabbits / 89, 96-97, 100-101 (see also *hares*)
    raccoons / 65, 74, 94, 98, 110
    reptiles / 89
    rodents / 92, 95, 98
    skunks / 74, 94, 98, 102-103

snakes / 58, 62, 72-73, 81, 91-92, 97, 102
squirrels / 55, 58, 89-90, 96, 101-102
turkeys / 84, 90, 103
wolves / 96
Antell, Steve / 147
Appalachian Long Distance Hikers Association / 141
Appalachian Mountain Club (see *AMC*)
Appalachian Mountain Gear (website) / 160
Appalachian Mountain Supply (sleeping pads) / 157, 160
Appalachian National Scenic Trail / 19, 148
Appalachian Trail Conference (ATC) / 14-15, 18-20, 29, 85,
    110, 113, 137-38, 140, 142, 147, 149, 171
    Board of Managers for / 14
    Regional Offices of / 138
Appalachian Trail Maintaining Clubs / 138, 137-42 (see also
    individual clubs)
Appalachian Trailway News / 19, 30
Arden, NY / 144
Armitage Hardware (website for Coleman) / 160
Artiach (sleeping pads) / 157
Asolo (boots) / 40, 154
AT Comprehensive Plan / 21
Atkins, VA / 143, *169*
Atway Carey, Ltd. (first aid kits) / 78
Audubon Society / 15, 148
Avery, Myron / 18, 21
Avid Outdoor (sleeping pads) / 157

B

Backcountry Outfitters (camping store) / 159
Backcountry Gear Limited (website) / 160
Backcountry Store (website) / 160
Backpacker magazine / 41, 78, 151
Bake Oven Knob, PA / 140, *166*
Bald Mountain, NC / 23, *170*
Baldpate Mountain, ME / 21, *163*
bank debit cards / 122 (see also *money*)

Barnes, Christy MacKaye / 149
Bastain, VA / 143, *169*
bathing / 111-12, 120 (see also *hygiene*)
batteries / 60, 112
Baxter Peak, ME / 21, 40, *162*
Baxter State Park, ME / *162*
Bear Mountain State Park, NY / 22, *165*
Beauty Spot, TN / 23, *170*
Beaver Tree Camp Kitchens (website) / 160
Bennington, VT / 144, *164*
Bibler Tents / 152
Big Bald, TN/NC / 12, *170*
Big Island, VA / 144
Big Wilson Stream, ME / 21, *162*
Bigelow Mountain, ME / 21, *162*
bivys / 52, 56, 58
Black Horse Gap, VA / 139, *169*
blackberries / 119
Bland, VA / 143, *169*
Blood Mountain, GA / 23, *171*
Blue Mountain Eagle Climbing Club / 140, *166*
Blue Ridge / 12, 19, 22, *166-68*
Blue Ridge Summit, PA / 144
Blue Sky Kitchen (website) / 160
Bly Gap, NC / 23, 138, *171*
BMO (camping store) / 159
Boiling Springs, PA / 144, *166*
Boonesboro, MD / 144
boots / 26, 32, 35, 39-43, 48, 58, 70, 120, 154, 156 (see also
    shoes)
Branchville, NJ / 144
Brandywine Valley Outing Club / 140, *166*
Brooks, Maurice / 14
Bruce, Dan "Wingfoot" / 61
Bunker Hill, VT / 22, *164*
Burkittsville, MD / 144

C

calories / 81-84 (see also *nutrition*)
cameras / 61, 66 (see also *TV* and individual makers' names)
Camp Trails (packs) / 51, 151
Campbell's (soup mixes) / 85
campfires (see *fires*)
The Camping Source (website) / 160
Campmor (website) / 160
campsites / 94, 103, 127
candles / 63, 65-66
Canon (cameras) / 66
Caratunk, ME / 145, *162*
Carolina Mountain Club / 138, *170*
Cascade Designs (sleeping pads) / 54, 151, 157
Catawba, VA / 144
cash (see *money*)
cellular telephones / 62
Center Point Knob, PA / 140, *166*
Central and Southwest Virginia Office of the ATC / 138
Chairback Mountain, ME / 21, *162*
Charlottesville Chapter of PATC / 140
Chazin, Daniel D. / 147
Cheoah Bald, NC / 23, *170*
Cherokee National Forest, NC / 97, *170*
Cheshire, MA / 144, *164*
Chew, V. Collins / 14, 149
Clarks Valley, PA / 140, *166*
Clingman's Dome, GSMNP, NC / 12, 40, *170*
clothing / 26, 39-46, 53-54, 57, 65, 67, 70, 75-77, 106, 112, 114
    (see also *boots* and *shoes*)
Cloverdale, VA / 144
Coleman Exponent (packs, sleeping bags, stoves) / 40, 151, 155,
    158, 160
compass / 126, 127 (see also *navigation*)
Connecticut / 12, 21, 22, 110, 117, 141, 144, 150, 155, 159,
    164-65
cooking / 59, 60, 114, 118 (see also *food*)
cookpot / 49, 60, 72, 84

Cornwall Bridge, CT / 144, *165*
Cox, Maynard H. / 74
Crazy Creek Products, Inc. (sleeping pads) / 157
Creasy, John / 15
credit cards / 121, 123 (see also *money*)
crime / 105-106
Crocker Ridge, ME / 21, *167*
Crowley, Suzanne / 15
cryptosporidium / 86-87
Cube Mountain, NH / 22, *163*
Cumberland Valley / 22, *166*
cutlery / 62, 77, 86 (see also *utensils*)

D

Dalton, MA / 144, *164*
Damascus, VA / 139, 143, *169*
Dana Design (packs) / 151
Danner Shoe Mfg. Co. (boots) / 40, 154
Darlington Trail, PA / 140, *166*
Dartmouth CO Op (camping store) / 159
Dartmouth Outing Club / 141, *163*
Darvill, Dr. Fred T., Jr. / 73-74, 149
Data Book / 85, 147
Davenport Gap, NC / 138, *170*
Delaware / 12, 22, 140-41, 144, 159, *166*
Delaware Water Gap NRA / 22, 144, *165*
derelicts / 56, 105-106
Derrick Knob Shelter, GSMNP, TN/NC / 98, 170
diet / 81-83, 93, 95-98, 101 (see also *food* and *nutrition*)
Dismal Branch, VA / 22, *168-69*
Doyle, Warren / 67
Dr. Bronner's Peppermint 18-in-1 Pure Castile Soap / 111-12, 114
Dragons Tooth, VA / 22, *168-69*
Duncannon, PA / 144, *166*
DuPont (insulation) / 52
Duracell (flashlights) / 64
Dynamed (snakebite kits) / 73

E

Eastern Mountain Sports (razors, tents, boots, sleeping bags) / 112, 152, 154, 156
eBay Auctions (website) / 160
Elk Park, NC / 143
emergencies / 29, 62, 73-74, 77, 85, 123 (see also *injuries*)
environment / 18, 20, 29, 59-60, 77, 90, 92, 113, 115, 117, 119-20, 148
erosion / 14, 43, 119-20
Erwin, TN / 143, *170*
Eureka! (tents) / 153
Eureka Camping Center (website) / 160
exhaustion / 48, 76-77 (see also *fatigue*)
Exstream Water Technologies (water filters) / 88, 158

F

fabrics / 41-43, 51-53, 56-58, 60-61, 64-65, 73, 76, 88, 91, 101, 112, 119 (see also *shells*)
Falls Village, CT / 144, *164*
fatigue / 30-31, 69, 76, 87, 120 (see also *exhaustion*)
Feathered Friends (sleeping bags) / 156
feces / 113-14, 119
Field Guide to North American Trees / 15
Field Guide to North American Wildflowers / 15
A Field Guide to the Birds East of the Rockies / 15
fills (see *insulation*)
financial / 121 (see also *money*)
fires / 47, 59-60, 65, 72, 76, 118
first aid / 42, 49, 69, 70-74, 78-79 (see also *injury* and *illness*)
First Essential (first aid kits) / 78
First Need (water filters) / 88
Fisher, Ron / 149
Five Ten Co. (boots) / 41, 154
Flack, James M. and Hertha E. / 147
Fletcher, Colin / 148
Fontana Dam, NC / 23, 143, *170*
food / 28, 30, 37-38, 59, 65, 81-86, 88, 148 (see also *cooking*)

poisoning from / 86
· sack for / 65, 85, 86, 94, 95, 98
Fort Montgomery, NY / 144
Foster, Charles H. W. / 19, 147
Fox Gap, PA / 141, *166*
Franconia Notch, NH / 22, *163*
Freeman Industries (toiletry kits) / 112
Front Royal, VA / 135, 144, *167*
Frozen Knob, TN / 23, *170*
fuel / 30, 49, 59-60, 65, 86 (see also *stoves*)

G

garbage bags / 65 (see also *plastic bags*)
Garmont USA (boots) / 154
Garuda (tents) / 153
Gatewood, Granny / 39
GearFind (website) / 160
General Delivery / 82 (see also *Post Office*)
General Ecology (water filters) / 88, 158
Georgia / 21, 23, 25, 55, 72, 91, 121, 138, 143, 149-50, 158, *170-71*
Georgia Appalachian Trail Club / 138, *171*
giardia lamblia / 86-88
Gifford Woods State Park, VT / 22, *164*
Glencliff, NH / 145, *163*
Global Positioning System (GPS) / 62
Gooding, Dunham / 31
Gorham, NH / 145, *163*
Gorp.com / 160
government / 18-20, 120, 127
GPS (see *Global Positioning System*)
Grafton Notch, ME/NH / 141, *163*
Grayson Highlands State Park, VA / 22, 132, *169*
Great Smokies National Park / 23
Great Smoky Mountains National Park (GSMNP) / 23, 97
Great Smoky Mountains / 12, 93-94, 96, 99, 113
Green Mountain Club / 18, 141, *164*

Green Mountains / 12, 22, *164*
Greenleaf Hut / 100, *163*
GSMNP (see *Great Smoky Mountains National Park*)
guide books / 15, 19, 21, 45, 123, 125, 127, 150

H

Hampton, TN / 143
Hanover, NH / 145, *163*
A Happy Camper (website) / 160
Harpers Ferry, WV / 19, 144, 148-49, *167*
Hi-Tec Sports / 40, 154
High Country Outdoor Products (sleeping pads) / 157
hiking clubs / 137-42, *162-71* (see also individual clubs)
hiking sticks / 65, 67, 92
history / 12-19, 22, 62, 105, 127, 137
Hog Camp Gap, VA / 22, *168*
Hogback Ridge, TN / 23, *170*
honor system / 118
Hot Springs, NC / 143, *170*
Hudson Highlands / 22, *165*
hunting / 89, 93, 97, 100
hygiene / 70, 76, 111-14, 119

I

Illinois A.T. Club / 142
illness / 69, 74, 77, 86-87 (see also *infection* and *injury*)
Indiana Camp (first aid kits) / 78-79
infection / 71, 73-74, 87
injuries / 29, 26, 31-33, 42-43, 48, 60, 69-75, 77-78 (see also
    illness)
insects / 55, 57-58, 67, 75-76, 94, 102-103, 128
insulation (fill) / 51-52, 54
Integral Designs (tents, sleeping bags) / 153, 156
International Appalachian Trail / 142
iodine / 86-88
Iron Mountain, TN / 23, *170*

J

Jack Wolfskin (packs, sleeping bags) / 152, 156
JanSport, Inc. (packs) / 51, 152
JMS Tooling (website) / 160
jogging / 32
    shoes / 39, 42
    shorts / 44
Johns Hollow / 22, *168*
Johnson, President Lyndon B. / 19
journal / 59
Journal of the American Institute of Architects / 17

K

Kamp-Zeek (lanterns) / 66
Katadyn (pocket filters) / 88, 158
Katahdin / 12, 21, 25, 40, 49, 104, 141, *162*
Katahdin Stream / 21, *162*
Kelly Knob, GA / 23, *171*
Kelty, Inc. / 51, 152-53, 156
Kent, CT / 144, *165*
Kent Pond, VT / 22, *164*
Keystone Trails Association / 141
Killington, VT / 145, *164*
Kinsman Notch, NH / 22, 141, *163*
Kirkhams Outdoor Products (website) / 160
Kittatinny Mountain Ridge / 22, *165*
knives / 35, 62-63, 71, 86
Kondos Outdoors (website) / 160
Knorr (soup mixes) / 85

L

L.L.Bean, Inc. (catalog) / 40-41, 152, 156
LA Sportiva USA (boots) / 41, 154
Lakes of the Clouds Hut (White Mountains) / 119
Lambert, Darwin / 148

Lehigh Furnace Gap, PA / 140, *166*
Lick Skillet Hollow, VA / 22, *169*
Limelight (candles) / 66
Linden, VA / 144, *167*
Lipton (food) / 84
litter / 118 (see also *waste*)
Little Gap, PA / 140, *167*
Logue, Victoria and Frank / 147
Lost Spectacles Gap, VA / 22, *169*
Lowa Boot, LLC / 154
Lowe Alpine System (packs) / 152
Lower Appalachian Trail Association / 142
Lyme Center, NH / 145

M

MacKay, Benton / 17, 21, 149
mail / 58, 81-83, 85, 121 (see also *Post Office*)
Maine / 12-13, 18, 21, 91, 99-100, 102-103, 108, 112, 119, 127, 141-42, 145, 149-50, 152, 157, *162-63*
Maine Appalachian Trail Club / 141
Mallory (flashlights) / 63
Manchester Center, VT / 145, *164*
maps / 14, 45, 62, 123, 124, 125, 127, 149-50, 161-171
Maret, Darrell / 149
Marmot Mountain (sleeping bags) / 156
Marshall, Ann / 149
Maryland / 21-22, 140, 144, 150, *166-67*
Massachusetts / 21-22, 91, 141, 144, 150, *164*
Master Tree Finder / 16, 148
mattresses / 54 (see *sleeping, pads*)
Matts Creek, VA / 22
Max Patch, TN / 12, 23, *170*
McNett Aquamira Water Treatment / 88
medical kits / 78 (see also *first aid kits*)
medicine
    acetaminophen / 79 (*Tylenol*)
    antibiotics / 74-76

antiseptics / 69, 71, 79
aspirin / 69, 74, 75, 79
Imodium (brand of *loperamide HCL*) / 79
loperamide HCL / 79 (*Imodium*)
Tylenol (brand of *acetaminophen*) / 74, 79
Mendenhall, Ruth Dyar / 148
mental conditioning / 25-29, 31
Merrell Performance Footwear (boots) / 155
microorganisms / 86-88, 114 (see also specific organisms)
Mid Atlantic Regional Office of the ATC / 138
Miller, Dorcas S. / 148
Minox (camera) / 66
moisture / 41, 52, 54, 57, 127, 128 (see also *water*)
money / 36, 40, 65, 121 (see also *credit cards*)
Monson, ME / 108, 109, 145, *162*
Montane (website) / 160
Montebello, VA / 144
months / 14, 19, 26, 27, 28, 29, 31, 35, 45, 86, 118
    April / 25, 53
    August / 18, 53, 141
    February / 100
    July / 49, 53
    March / 18, 25, 53
    May / 16, 74
    October / 19, 99
    September / 25, 99, 148
    spring / 25, 27, 49, 57, 98, 149
    summer / 27, 28, 44, 56, 57, 75, 96, 98, 99, 101
    winter / 52, 98, 101
Montrail, Inc. (boots) / 41, 155
Moosineer (website) / 160
Moonstone (sleeping pads) / 157
Moss Tents / 153
Mount Washington, NH / 145, *163*
Mountain Zone (website) / 160
mountains / 11-15, 17-18, 20-22, 25-26, 29, 31, 35, 40-
    41, 47, 49, 53, 57, 73, 86, 88-89, 91, 93, 95-98, 100,
    112, 119, 121, 138, 140-41, 144, 148-49, 152-60 (see also
    specific mountains and peaks)

Mountain Club of Maryland / 140, *166*
Mountain Hardwear (tents, sleeping pads) / 153, 156-57
Mountain Safety Research (MSR water filters) / 88, 158
Mountaineering Medicine / 73, 149
Mountainsmith, Inc. (packs) / 152
Mount Washington / 21, 119, *163*
Mount Rogers Appalachian Trail Club / 139, *169*
Moxie Bald Mountain, ME / 21, *162*
Muesser, Roland / 31
Myles Recreational Accessories (website) / 160

N

Nahmakanta Lake, ME / 21, *162*
Nantahala
    National Forest / 97, *170-71*
    Hiking Club / 138, *170*
    Mountains / 12, 23, *170-71*
National Park Service (NPS) / 20, 94, 100, 148, 171
National Scenic Trail / 19
National Scenic Trails Act / 19
Natural Bridge Appalachian Trail Club / 139, *168*
navigation / 62, 123 (see also *Global Positioning System*)
Neels Gap, GA / 23, *171*
Nesuntabunt Lake, ME / 21, *162*
New Balance (boots) / 40
New England Regional Office of the ATC / 138
New Hampshire / 19, 21, 119, 138, 141, 145, 150,
    152, 154, 156, 158, 159, *163-64*
New Jersey / 18, 21, 22, 100, 110, 117, 141, 144, 150, *165-66*
New York / 18, 21, 22, 91, 101, 106, 110, 117, 141, 144,
    148, 150-51, *164-65*
New York-New Jersey Trail Conference / 18, 141
Nike (boots) / 40, 155
Nikon (cameras) / 66
No Business Knob, TN / 23, *170*
Noall Tents / 153
Norquest Innovation Corp. (website) / 160

North Adams, MA / 144, *164*
North Carolina / 12, 15, 19, 21, 23, 91, 95, 97, 100, 112,
    138-39, 143, 150, 159, *168-70*
North Chapter of PATC / 140
North Face (packs, tents) / 51, 152, 153
North Florida Snakebite Treatment Center / 74
North Woodstock, NH / 145, *163*
Northern Shenandoah Valley Chapter of PATC / 140
Northward Bound (website) / 160
Norwich, VT / 145
nutrition (see also *food*)
    carbohydrates / 83
    fat / 83-84
    protein / 83

O

Old Dominion Appalachian Trail Club / 139, *168*
Olympus (cameras) / 66
Optimus (stoves) / 158
Outdoor Club of Virginia Tech / 139
Outdoor Experience (website) / 160
Outdoor World (website) / 160

P

PATC (see *Potomac Appalachian Trail Club*)
Pack Shack Adventures, Inc. (camping store) / 159
packs / 29, 32, 40, 47-51, 57-61, 64-65, 75, 78, 82-
    85, 88, 93, 94, 106, 112-14, 118, 151-52
    center of gravity for carrying / 49-51
    covers for / 64-65
pain / 42, 47, 48, 70-74, 102 (see also *injuries*)
Palmerton, PA / 144
parasites / 86-87 (see also *microorganisms*)
Pawling, NY / 144, *165*
Pearisburg, VA / 143, *169*
Pemadumcook Lake, ME / 21, *162*

Pennsylvania / 19, 21-22, 91, 98-99, 101, 106, 117, 138-41, 144, 148, 150, 159, *165-67*
Pentax (cameras) / 66
perspiration / 41, 70, 77, 127 (see also *moisture*)
Peterson, Roger Tory / 15, 148
Philadelphia Trail Club / 140, *166*
physical conditioning / 27, 31-32, 47, 72, 74, 77 (see also *fatigue*)
Piedmont Appalachian Trail Hikers / 139, *169*
Pine Grove, PA / 144
Pine Grove Furnace State Park, PA / 139-40, *166*
Pine Swamp Shelter / 139, *169*
plastic bags / 64, 86 (see also *garbage bags* and *Ziploc bags*)
pocketknife / 62-63, 86 (see also *knives*)
Port Clinton, PA / 144, *166*
Post Offices, U.S. / 82, 85, 127, 143-45
Potomac Appalachian Trail Club / 140, *167*
Powell Mountain, GA / 23, *171*
Prater, Yvonne / 148
prescriptions / 87
Primus/Suunto USA (stoves) / 158
privies / 113, 137
protozoa / 86-87 (see also *microorganisms*)
Punchbowl Mountain, VA / 22, *168*
PUR (water filters) / 88, 159

R

rabies / 74, 75, 90, 96, 103
Raichle Outdoor (boots) / 40, 155
Rainbow Stream / 21
Rangeley, ME / 145, *162*
Rausch Creek / 140
Recreational Equipment, Inc. (REI) / 78, 152, 153, 157
Reeds Gap, VA / 139
REI / 51, 73, 78, 79, 152, 153, 156
rest / 11, 27, 54, 73, 119
restaurants / 85, 121-22
rivers / 12-13, 21-23, 62-63, 139-41, 159

Androscoggin River / 21, *163*
Connecticut River / 22, *163*
Delaware River / 22, 141, *165*
French Broad River / 12, 23, *170*
Housatonic River / 12, *165*
Kennebec River / 12, 21, *162*
Little Tennessee River / 23, *170*
Nantahala River / 23, *170-71*
New River / 13, *168-69*
Nolichucky River / 12, 23, *170*
Penobscot River, / 12, 21, *162*
Pigeon River / 23, *170*
Potomac River / 12, 22, *167*
Shenandoah River / 22, *167*
Susquehanna River / 12, 22, 140, *165-66*
Tye River / 139, *168*
Watauga River / 12, *169*
Roan Mountain Massif, TN/NC / 23, *170*
Roanoke Appalachian Trail Club / 139, *168-69*
Rockfish Gap, VA / 22, 139, *168*
Rockfish Gap Outfitters (camping store) / 159
Rockport Co., The (boots) / 41
rope / 65, 94-95
Round Bald, TN/NC / 12, 131, *170*
rules / 29, 82, 115, 117-20 (see also *government*)

S

Saddleback Mountain, ME / 21, *162*
Safe Water Anywhere (water filters) / 159
safety / 106, 110 (see also *crime*)
Sages Ravine, MA / 141, *164*
Salisbury, CT / 144, *164*
Salomon North America (boots) / 40, 155
Salt Log Gap, VA / 22, *168*
sanitation / 111, 114-15 (see also *hygeine*)
Nelson, Senator Gaylord / 19
Shaffer, Earl V. / 149

shell / 52, 53, 60, 86, 88 (see also *fabric*)
shelters / 26, 40-41, 55-56, 59, 63, 65, 75, 87-88, 90, 94, 98-99, 103, 106, 108, 110, 113-14, 118, 120, 127, 137 (see also *tents*)
Shenandoah National Park / 22, 93, 94, 150, *168*
shoes (see also *boots*)
    sandals / 41
    sneakers / 39
sickness / 86 (see also *illness*)
Sierra Designs (tents, sleeping bags) / 51, 153, 156
Silers Bald, GSMNP / 99, *170*
Sinking Creek, VA / 22, *168*
Skyline Drive / 19, 22, 73, *167-68*
sleeping
    bags / 26, 51, 53-54, 58-60, 64-65, 75, 77, 156
    gear / 57
    pads / 43, 50, 54, 78-79, 114, 157
    pillows / 28, 54
Slumberjack (sleeping bags, sleeping pads) / 156-57
Smarts Mountains, NH / 22, *163*
Smoky Mountains Hiking Club / 138, *170*
snakebite / 72, 73, 74, 92 (see also *emergencies*)
Snow Bird Mountains / 23, *170*
South Egremont, MA / 144
Snow Leopard Mountain Sports (website) / 160
South Mountain / 22, *167*
South Mountain, PA / 144
South Pomfret, VT / 145
Southern Shenandoah Valley Chapter of PATC / 140
Spivey Gap, NC / 138, 139, *170*
Springer Mountain, GA / 21, 23, 25, 40, 49, 121, 138, *171*
springs / 19, 23, 87, 111-12, 114, 138, 140, 143-44, 159
Standing Indian Mountain, NC / 23, *170-71*
Stecoah Gap, GA / 95, *171*
Stern, Roger / 15
Sterns, Inc. (sleeping pads) / 157
Stormville, NY / 144
stoves / 30, 49, 59-60, 118
Stover Creek, GA / 23, *171*

stoves / 37, 59-60, 84, 158 (see also *fuel*)
Stratton, ME / 145, *162*
streams / 21, 25-26, 41, 58, 66, 77, 87, 98, 99, 111, 114 (see
    also *rivers*)
stuff sacks / 53-54, 58
Suches, GA / 143, *171*
Sugarloaf Mountain, ME / 18, *162*
SunnyRec Corp. (sleeping pads) / 157
Susquehanna Appalachian Trail Club / 140, *166*
Swiss Army (knives) / 62-63, 71
switchbacks / 119-20
SympaTex Technologies (fabrics) / 53

T

Tar Jacket Ridge, VA / 22, *168*
Tecnica USA (boots) / 155
Tennessee / 15, 21, 23, 91, 97, 100, 138-39, 143, 150, *169-71*
Tennessee Eastman Hiking Club / 139, *170*
Tennessee, North Carolina and Georgia Office of the ATC / 138
tents / 26, 30, 55-59, 61, 64-65, 75, 99-100, 110, 114, 119,
    152-53
The Appalachian National Scenic Trail / 19
The Appalachian Trail Conference Member Handbook / 19
The Appalachian Trail: A Journey of Discovery / 128, 147
The Appalachian Trail: Onward to Katahdin / 128
The Lessinger Group (insulation) / 52
The North Face (packs, tents, sleeping bags) / 51, 152-53, 156
Therm-A-Rest (air mattresses) / 54
Thoreau, Henry David / 17, 149
Tidewater Appalachian Trail Club / 139, *168*
toilet paper / 49, 65, 112-13
toiletries / 112 (see also *hygiene*)
Trail clubs / 20, 124, 137-42, *162-71*
Trail Data / 21
Trail markings / 100-101, 119, 123, 125
trash / 114, 118 (see *waste*)
Tray Mountain, GA / 23, *171*

Trekker (first aid kits) / 78
Tri-County Corner / 140, *166*
Troutville, VA / 143-44
TV / 61 (see also *cameras*)
Tyringham, MA / 144, *164*
Tyro, VA / 144

U

Ultima (first aid kits) / 78
Unaka Mountain, TN / 23, *170*
Underfoot / 14
Unionville, NY / 144, *165*
U.S Department of the Interior / 19 (see also *rules*)
U.S. Navy SEAL Supply Store (website) / 160
utensils / 60, 78, 88, 111, 114, 119 (see also *cutlery*)

V

Vasque (boots) / 40-41, 155
VauDe Sports, Inc. (stoves) / 158
Venture Outdoors (website) / 160
Vermont / 12-13, 15, 18, 21-22, 58, 99, 101, 103, 113, 141, 144-45, 148, 150, 154, *163-64*
Vernier, Dr. Vernon G. / 72
Vernon, NJ / 144, *165*
Vickery, Jim Dale / 149
violations / 20, 118-20 (see also *rules*)
Virginia / 12-13, 19, 21-22, 73, 82, 90-91, 99, 101-102, 112, 138-40, 143-44, 150, 159, *167-70*
volunteers / 120 (see also *hiking clubs*)

W

W. L. Gore & Associates (fabrics) / 52-53
Walden / 17, 149
Walrus, Inc. (tents) / 153
waste / 111, 113-14, 118

water / 12-13, 20, 22, 27, 30, 37, 41, 48, 52, 54, 56-57, 59, 64-65, 70, 72, 75-77, 81, 84, 86-88, 91-92, 111-14, 119-20, 137, 139, 144, 148, 159 (see also *moisture*)
Waterman, Laura and Guy / 148
Watts, May Theilgaard / 16, 148
Wayah Bald, NC / 23, *170*
Waynesboro, VA / 144, *168*
weapons / 97, 102 (see also *crime*)
weather / 23, 26, 28-29, 31-32, 35, 41, 49, 52-53, 56-60, 62, 64, 69, 70-72, 75-78, 83, 85, 90, 94, 100-101, 103, 110, 119-20, 127-28, 137, 147
websites / 38, 52-53, 125-26 137-42, 151-60
weight / 14, 16, 30, 32, 35, 39, 41, 43, 47, 50, 56-61, 63, 67, 78, 83, 95, 112
Welch, Major William / 18
Wesser, NC / 138, *170*
West Hartford, VT / 145
West Virginia / 19, 21, 22, 137, 140, 144, *167-69*
West Virginia Chapter of PATC / 140
Whisperlite (stoves) / 59
White Mountains, NH / 21, 23, *163*
wildflowers / 11, 15, 32, 119, 148
Wilmington Trail Club / 141
Wind Gap, PA / 140-41, 144, *166*
Wolverine (boots, shoes) / 155
World Wide Poison Bite Information Center / 74
WPC Brands, Inc. (water filters) / 88, 159

Y

Yahoo.com (website) / 160
York Hiking Club / 140, *166*

Z

Zip Ztove (stoves) / 60
ZZ Manufacturing (stoves) / 158

About
the Author

Jan Curran, a native New Yorker, **Jan D. Curran**
holds a baccalaureate degree
from the University of Vermont and a masters degree from Niagara
University. He hiked the entire Appalachian Trail following his retirement from the Army. Anticipating that the hike would be a tran-
sition vehicle to assist in making the psychological adjustment necessitated by retirement, Curran quickly found himself addressing
more profound issues. The result was a reordering of the basic priorities in his life. This experience became the basis for his widely
acclaimed books, *The Appalachian Trail: A Journey of Discovery*
and *The Appalachian Trail: Onward to Katahdin.*

Since hiking the Trail, Curran has traveled and lectured extensively about his experiences and about hiking the Appalachian Trail.
He frequently revisits selected portions of the Trail. In this book he
shares rare insights into the psychological aspects of long-distance
hiking as well as providing tips to help make anyone's visit to the
AT a memorable experience.

Curran currently makes his home in Naples, Florida, where
proximity to the Gulf of Mexico provides ample opportunity to
indulge in his second passion, sailing.

The Appalachian Trail Series

by Jan D. Curran

The Appalachian Trail: How To Prepare For & Hike It
ISBN (softcover): 1-56825-050-9 / $14.95

The Appalachian Trail: A Journey of Discovery
ISBN (softcover): 0-935834-66-4 / $12.95

The Appalachian Trail: Onward to Katahdin
ISBN (softcover): 1-56825-072-X / $14.95

— How To Order —

— **Phone.** Call Book Clearing House toll free at 1-800-431-1579 (Visa, MasterCard, American Express and Discover)

— **Online.** Find your best price of all the online booksellers by comparing prices at http://www.allbookstores.com

— **Your local bricks-and-mortar bookseller.** Ask for the specific titles/ISBN numbers listed above.